Diary of a Schizophrenic

2nd Edition

Paul Fearne

chipmunkapublishing
the mental health publisher

Paul Fearne

All rights reserved, no part of this publication may be reproduced by any means, electronic, mechanical photocopying, documentary, film or in any other format without prior written permission of the publisher.

>Published by
>Chipmunkapublishing
>United Kingdom

http://www.chipmunkapublishing.com

Copyright ©2017 Paul Fearne

ISBN   978-1-78382-382-6

PREFACE

It is with great pleasure I write the preface to this, the second edition of my diary. There has been much that has happened in the interim. This diary was my first published book. It was to go on and be launched at the 2010 Melbourne Writers Festival. At the time I was interviewed on Radio National's show 'All in the Mind' around the country. This was to start a journey I never expected.

My second book, A Schizophrenic on Artaud, was launched at Readings in Carlton. I was during this time to appear at the Emerging Writers Festival. Highlights from my performance were broadcast on ABC News 24 as part of the 'Big Ideas' show.

I then became co-host of a radio show called 'Poet's Corner' on 3CR community radio. It was part of the 'Brainwaves' show, for and about those suffering from mental illness.

My third book, A Schizophrenic to Strindberg, was launched at Readings on the Melbourne University campus. I was unwell at the time, and was given special leave from hospital to attend the launch.

And my fourth book was my PhD which was published by Scholars Press. I launched the PhD at the North Melbourne Public Library.

So I am pleased to announce, since the publication of the first edition of this diary, I did indeed go on to do my PhD! Much hard work, but these things always are.

Just a quick mention concerning topographical matters in the book. I have left some grammatical errors in the text to lend it some authenticity. I was writing during a psychotic episode, so to leave these in seemed pertinent. But on the whole, surprisingly, the grammar is fine.

Thank you for your interest in this book!

And remember, 'Schizophrenia is not a diagnosis, it's an adventure!'

Diary of a Schizophrenic

INTRODUCTION

This diary is a record of a journey from illness to recovery. In 1998 I experienced a schizophrenic episode. I was set upon by a litany of delusions that were to debilitate me for some time. During this episode, I kept a diary – the work which you now have. The diary moves from a pre-occupation with the manifestations of my illness, to a more sober account of a life that was regaining the semblance of normalcy. It was refreshing for me to finally read to the later half of the journal, which show increasing levels of sanity and degrees of equanimity.

There is in this diary a pre-occupation with writing and the desire to undertake further study at a postgraduate level. I can report that I went on, after this episode, to do a Masters degree in philosophy, and am currently undertaking a PhD in the same discipline. A value of this diary I believe is that it can give hope to those who are suffering from schizophrenia. Not only did I go on to these degrees, but I also became president of the University of Melbourne Philosophy Club, as well as postgraduate representative in philosophy at LaTrobe University, became a published poet and philosopher, and even became married. If one survives the vicissitudes of schizophrenia, one may be able to go on to achieve one's goals.

Another intrinsic value of this diary is that it allows someone who is not schizophrenic and who reads the book to gain some insight into what it must be like to actually experience an episode. One enters the world of the schizophrenic as it were, and sees the complexities that the experience presents a person.

The delusions that this volume presents the reader with are indeed fascinating. I was to experience the delusion that sound and light could actually enter my mind and damage it in some way. I thought that 'portions' of my 'being' would leave my body at certain moments, such as getting up from a chair. The diary also details other pre-occupations.

Paul Fearne

Ruminations on philosophy, literature and art abound, and are intertwined with the strange irrationalities that the schizophrenic mind exhibits.

The names in this diary have been changed to protect the identities of the people in it, although surprisingly the things I have said about them are mostly positive (surprising given the experience I was having).

I hope you find the following thoughts of interest.

■

DIARY

I wonder if I'll be able to write like I once did. After all that has happened to me and my mind. Will the store of ideas suddenly dry up? I sincerely hope not. For a start I'm not too sure that I like this laptop. The keyboard doesn't seem to suit my style of writing. The sound effects are also getting a little bit on my nerves.

Somehow I think that my ability to write my memoirs has left me. It doesn't feel like the flow is there. I guess having you're emotions destroyed is very crippling to the creative process. Anyway, we'll see how I go in my next assignment. I have a feeling it won't be of that B plus standard, which is a shame because it was quite a pleasant surprise to find that mark on my last paper. I hadn't scored a B plus for quite sometime. Oh what am I thinking of, of course I'll get a B plus, I should be aiming for an A after the progression my grades have taken; C, B minus then a B plus. The logical progression is an A. Well enough of this preoccupation with grades.

I'm getting the desire back to study and research, but I feel my mind is simply not up to the task any more. Its so frustrating, I just simply can't feel my emotions anymore. There's no sadness, no happiness, no response from my emotions whatsoever. There also seems to be no critical responsiveness from mind. When I read a piece of my work there isn't that critical faculty there anymore, there's just this blank emotionless slate which I peer into. Oh cruel fate, to cast upon one such as myself this burden of living without emotions. How does one live when there is no pleasure in anything! I used to live with a very acute sense of emotion, feeling everything that happened to me with a strong emotional punch. This is more than one person is able to stand.

I think my one dream is to once again capture the joys of writing. To become once again immersed in the art of words, the sculpture which is language. I think its still in me somewhere, despite all I've lost. Even though my mind is not functioning with the same emotional intensity I feel I still have something to contribute in the way of words. What else have I to do with my time? It's a question of either pacing around the house all day going out of my mind or doing something constructive with my time. What to write about though? All my interests are dead within the husk which is my body. The creative juice has ceased to flow a long time ago. Thoughts which I once had have now abandoned me. The lofty heights of intellectual prowess which I once enjoyed no longer inhabit my mind. Those wonderful flights into the realms of abstract thought which were my life-blood are now just memories of a long forgotten age.

How can I continue with a life that is so dead in feelings? My emotional intensity was the well-spring from which my life drew its meaning, and now that it is gone I can do nothing but mourn its passing. There is such a large part of me which is gone that I sometimes feel that I will never recover. There have been a number of defining moments in my life, but the day I lost my emotions is perhaps the day I will regret the most. How can this happen to one so young and so full of life? I thought such tragedy was only written about by the Greeks, not lived in this modern era. The ability to write poetry was one of the sweet joys of life that gave hope to a sometimes troubled existence. But it was those troubles which gave life its edge and vitality. To enjoy a sunset after the tumult of everyday living is a joy I guess I will rarely live again. I remember once watching a documentary on one of the great musicians. It described how in the later parts of his life the creative fire began to die within his bosom. I remember it clearly because it was about the same time I was set upon by my troubles. It seems that those of us who burn the brightest are the same who die the coldest deaths. To know the exhilaration of heightened thought and then to watch it slowly slip away is something almost unbearable. I think I know how the supernova star feels.

To live such a cold emotional life is something I never thought would happen to me. How can anyone imagine the total decimation of their inner world? We all go living life taking for granted those parts of ourselves which are dearest to us. It is only when they are gone that we truly miss the subtle impact which they have upon our lives. Well hardly subtle when they have been completely taken away.

I'm trying to understand how what is happening to me can possibly happen at all. How does a persons mind become so fragile and exposed the outside world that to live is take a leap into a sea of daggers, each one stabbing the fabric of your being. How can light pass from a person's eye to sear their very mind? It's obviously some sort of hypersensitivity. But how can it destroy parts of that mind. It seems an impossibility; a scary impossibility. My CT scan has cleared me of any structural damage to my brain, but my mind is still decimated. I still converse and write quite freely, but it is within the very perceptions which the mind makes which is impinged upon most dramatically. Not only does light affect my mind, but somehow so does sound. Even while I'm writing this I know how crazy it sounds. It's like a freakish nightmare dreamt and then quickly forgotten. And it is like living a nightmare. How can sound damage a persons mind? How is that medically possible? I've neglected talking about this to anyone for fear of no one believing me, but I can't be the only person in the world who is suffering from such a thing. There must be someone else who has experienced a similar phenomena. To lose your emotions is something I would not wish upon anyone else, but there must be even a body of scientific knowledge somewhere that deals with this occurrence.

I think given a choice of professions I would dearly have loved to be an intellectual. I think it would have been a very rewarding life. A fine love of classical music and classic literature would have suited me quite well. Not to mention my passion for philosophy. I would have been a philosophy lecturer travelling the world giving lectures in a range of different topics. To sit for hours tucked away in a country retreat writing articles on my laptop would have been a joy. It would have suited my nature quite amicably. To use your mind in the pursuit of philosophical inquiry would have been a treat.

But listen to myself, I 'm talking as if my life is already over. Well I guess professionally it is for all intensive purposes. It's going to be a hard life watching all my friends take off into their own professions while I am stuck in the position in which I'm in. I really don't know how I'm going to live the rest of my life. I simply live from one day to the next, not even dreaming of the future, for now my future seems quite barren. It's not even a dark future, just a cold meaningless existence trudging through life with no fixed plans, just trying my best to survive. I never thought I'd be doing this, just surviving, but that's about the extent of it. No joy, no sadness, just the continual daily dramas as I watch my mind being whittled away. Nobody should be forced to live the life which I am leading. It's such a sterile existence that I'm at a loss to fully comprehend it. What makes it so much worse is the life that I used to lead, full of emotional intensity and intellectual capacity. I sometimes don't even have my memories to keep me company.

I really am at a loss as to what to do. This cold vacuity which is my existence has driven me to despair - no not even despair, for that's an emotion which I am no longer able to feel. There's just nothing, a cold blank! How does a person's life end up in such a state? There's nothing I can do to express the barrenness I feel, I've entered a realm were language can no longer follow. All I can do is talk in terms of lack, absence, non-existence. For a time all I was concerned about was what was going to happen to me after I died - but what about now. What about my life now! There's going to be no time to enjoy the securities of maturity. My adolescent life was very emotional, something of a roller coaster. Now I will never know what it feels like to be an adult. My life was cruelly cut down on the cusp of my manhood.

So what can I do? What positive step can be taken? Well I think I've exhausted all my options. There's nothing left to do but slowly fade away.

Another thing I find it very difficult to understand is how patting the cat affects me. Somehow touching the cat affects my mind directly. I can't explain exactly how, there's no reduction is mental faculties, its just a perceptual thing. My mind feels more enclosed if that makes any sense. It never lasts very long and can sometimes not even affect me at all, but when it does it is very annoying - no, more than annoying, very disconcerting. It's not enough that mind is exposed to light in the way it is, it's also exposed to my cat! In fact its quite frustrating, I finally felt as if my mind was coming along this morning, only to have it once again destroyed by simply patting the cat. Oh well, I guess this is my life, just glimpses of a normal life only to have them whisked away by either the strong light, cold drinks or the cat.

I just can't understand what is wrong with me. It seems as if parts of my very being just drop out of my body if I happen to turn suddenly. How is this possible? I was just starting to remember my religious convictions when all of a sudden it seemed as if my heart just went dead. It's like parts of my being just pop out of my body. I look to where my feelings once were and there is just an inky blackness, whereas before there was at passion and conviction. I find myself struggling with the words to describe exactly what happens.

Somehow my being has opened up and is exposed to the outside world - and is so tenuously linked with my body that it just removes itself whenever my momentum shifts direction. What does this mean, that the very fibres of a person's being can be affected somehow by gravity? It seems a nightmarish possibility, but this whole situation in which I find myself is so nightmarish that I'm hardly surprised.

I continually think of what will happen to me after I'm dead. I believe in God but I sometimes feel as if even he will be unable to save me. I remember the passion I once had for my religious convictions. It was my true love to read works such as *The Cloud of Unknowing* and *The Dark Night of the Soul*. They gave my life its direction and purpose - things which I now seem to be unable to find in life. I sometimes feel as if my life ended six months ago, but hopefully I will regain my passion for such works and God can show himself in my life. I've had some quite extraordinary brushes with the divine, and hopefully I will never forget them, and they will continue to shed light upon an otherwise bleak existence. I live from day to day, sometimes with no hope, and it's only the memories of what I was and how I felt about God that keep me going. My one fear now is that I will lead a life without the loving hand of God to show me some direction. I'm sure he will somehow find a way to enter into my life and give it some comfort.

It so frustrating that I seem to have lost the ability to appreciate beauty. It was once of the founding strengths of my life that I could take a walk in the late afternoon and appreciate the golden red sprays of light upon the clouds above. But for some reason I find myself unable to appreciate such beauties in nature. I think its linked to the lose of my emotive impetus. The two are no doubt linked somehow. To have been given the gift of such appreciation and then to have it torn away sometimes seems unbearable. Even the vision of the rolling green hills of Scotland has failed to move me. I never thought I could possibly live such a stale and lifeless existence. It's not enough that all my interests have been stolen away, but my appreciation of the beautiful has now been taken. It's quite enough to feel

Diary of a Schizophrenic

depressed about, but I can't even feel depressed anymore. That wonderful sorrow that filled my life, that supreme longing that led me to all the great spiritual texts has now deserted me, leaving nothing but a shell of a man to pick up the pieces of a shattered life.

We are vision filled
And in the silence nature speaks
Giving a certain solace
To those who have tallied long enough
To Hear the words once forgotten
But eternally embraced
In a dance that heralds day
To those who chose to stay

Oh hark that herald of the day
Who on pinions holds the clouds at bay
Giving hope to some who sleep
In dreams of life by heavens keep

Listen sweetly as we tell
Of things foretold by heavens bell
Slumber, slumber, we hear you say
Forget not love, it is the way
Of heart felt bliss we are no stranger
But as of late it's gone, no wager

I can't believe it, my life just continues its slide into oblivion. I was just taking a pleasant walk in the botanical gardens when I walked past a man shovelling sand into a wheelbarrow. My mind was immediately shattered so that I could hardly remember what I had been thinking. The grating sound had somehow impinged itself upon my fragile mind. It's so frustrating. I was just beginning to remember my life before the troubles when my thinking was disturbed in such a dramatic fashion.

Well there have been other developments in this pitiful life since last I wrote. It seems as if that part of my mind which takes a joy in books has been destroyed. All I did was turn on the light in one of the rooms and BAM it was gone. It was quite an interesting experience, because I distinctly remember looking at my bookshelf and thinking how wonderful the books I had bought were just before I walked into the room and turned the light on. Afterwards I went back to that same bookshelf and couldn't perceive the books as I had before. There was just a blank mind staring at me were once there had been a wonderful appreciation of books. Well I guess that was the final pleasure in my life destroyed. It seems as if that very same part of my mind that was destroyed is the same part that that takes an appreciation of prints and art works. I look at the prints which I have on my walls and I get absolutely no response whatsoever. What used to be a deep appreciation of a piece of art work has turn into a cold barren mind state. Not only that but even looking at pictures I get no response from. My mind is just a blank when it comes to anything visual. Even the TV fails to move me at all. I think I'm slowly but surely losing every part of my mind that meant anything to me. I thought things couldn't get any worse after my emotions were destroyed, but they have. To lose a love of books is perhaps more than I can tolerate. The only thing left that gave me any pleasure whatsoever. I remember lying in bed this morning mulling that fact over in my, and there was no single iota of an emotion response. I'd just lost the only thing keeping me going and there was no feeling whatsoever. I couldn't hold the thought long enough for it to really sink in.

I feel lower now than I ever imagined possible. No - I can't even feel low, all I do is exist; from one day to the next. There is no hope. Just today I was having coffee with dad and he began talking about his dreams for the future - and it struck me, I have no dreams, nothing to live for. The only reason there is for life is the slight chance God may still be with me. This is the only thing I live for. I feel no love, cannot even feel simple emotion, cannot even long for emotion - only envy those who have such things.

Diary of a Schizophrenic

My one dream is to be a writer. But I'm not sure my mind is up to it. Can one be a writer without emotions and with a slowly deteriorating mind? Just today I thought that I had finally lost my mind. There are just too many things which impinge themselves upon my consciousness that I fear it is only a matter of time before I do. Even looking at this computer screen is affecting my mind. And I just can't tell when something will effect it and just how dramatically. Can I become a writer? I think in all seriousness not. I've lost my imaginative faculty, a must for any aspiring writer. It's a shame because I once had quite a lively imagination. Couple that with quite a sharp intellect and penchant for emotional intensity and I guess I had quite a good life. But now it only makes it harder to live; to have once had such gifts and then to have them taken away so dramatically. One might say life was unfair.

I went to Lisa Kennedy's for dinner last night and it dawned on me just what I'm now missing out of life. My old friend Peter Kennedy was there and we had quite a dinner party. Just to see them converse and laugh amongst themselves in a way I never will be able to again was quite a saddening experience. They are all so full of life and passion that it was difficult for me to remain composed throughout the night. All I could keep thinking was how my life had finished while theirs had just began. They all had so much heart. I guess no one noticed my quite and reluctant composure as anything out of the ordinary. I truly admire them their life and vitality. When I think of how I spend my days and how they must spend theirs it makes me more than a little sad. To watch my mind being slowly whittled away is so frustrating at times such as this. I really missed the meaning of life over the past year. I forgot the basic fundamentals while I was reaching for the stars. Family and friends are the most important things which a person can have, and I threw away them all. But now that I can appreciate them again I've lost the ability to feel empathy from them.

My one regret now is that I'll never be able to become a writer. Secluded away writing books would have suited me perfectly. Long periods of writing punctuated by dinner and stimulating conversation with friends. I've lost the ability to converse on abstract topics, which is a real shame. I can't believe I won't get the opportunity to grow and mature with my friends. Their conversations have reached that adult level and all I can do is listen, I can't seem to join in. I guess I never was much of a conversationalist, but I had my moments.

Ah, I wish I had the ability again to master the use of words. To write poetry again is something I'll have to do. I actually enjoyed reading some Wordsworth today.

To have tasted the sweetness
Contained within a golden red cloud
And then to have it pale and fade
Is a tragedy none should bare
To have flown on the wings of thought
as they fly you over that many coloured land
And then to awake from the dream
as if it was never dreamt
Is a pain as none should bare

I was in a university today I went and visited the philosophy office, my old stomping grounds. I could almost remember back to the days when I used to study there and the great dreams I had for the future. It was painful to see the place now in the state in which I'm in. To know there is no hope of ever recovering my former enthusiasms and interests. I looked at some of the bookshelves in Ian Bradley's office, and I couldn't even feel that yearning anymore. My mind has just gone dead. It's something which I could have been; a university lecturer. And it pains me greatly that I'll never get the chance - I had a real talent. The university life would have suited me well. I can't even imagine anymore what it was like during those days, when my thoughts would sore to new philosophic heights. All the great philosophical questions I was interested in. It was a passion that I sorely miss. To lose a gift like that is not something one recovers from. It stays with a person the rest of their lives. I just can't

Diary of a Schizophrenic

believe it's over. There's nothing to do now but grind on. There is no meaning to this life anymore. Nothing to look forward to, no dreams or ambitions. I once had such things but now they're long gone. Oh how I miss them so. I can't even say to myself, well I'll just have to get on with life, because there seems no life to get on with. I can't even pretend like I had been doing. My mind has just lost all its power to create a life. Even after my life had ground to halt, I could still look at books and imagine that I was going to be an academic. But it's all over now. My life, my love of books, my passion for philosophy. Oh why has this happened to me? I've only just started life and its now over. I can't even console myself with the simpler things anymore. The beautiful day is no longer beautiful. My philosophic mind is dead, and all the joys it brought. I feel like I should be entering the final years of my life, having lived a gloriously fruitful life, but it simply isn't to be. How does one come to terms with such a situation? Is it possible? Well I think in my case not. My father keeps asking me what I'm to do with my life, what am I to say. I had dreams but they're now over. All I want to do is recapture my life again so I can go on and live the life I should be living.

I've just realised what my problem might be - why I am experiencing this condition. It is most likely a result of my time at Doncaster under Robert Blackburn. I feel now that I was subject to mind manipulation techniques, or brain washing. Everything that is happening to me is happening to my mind. And I'm pretty sure it has to do with Robert Blackburn's supposed "teachings". I've just bought a book called "recovery from cults" and reading it has made me realise just how manipulated I was.

My memory is sometimes very vague as to what happened at Doncaster, and I'm finding myself struggling to even write these few lines. It must be a result of the techniques he used on me. I've decided to see Dr Rachel Allen who has had some experience with people who have left Doncaster. Hopeful she will have a little bit of insight into exactly what goes on there. And maybe I can try and talk to her about some of my experiences there. Who knows it may even help me overcome this terrible condition I've developed.

I am so infuriated at the thought of having been brainwashed. My life is over before it eve began just because that place and that teacher. No I wouldn't call him a teacher, more like a manipulator. Hopefully I can recall some of what happened to me and it will somehow unlocked that part of mind which holds my feelings and emotions. I will write about them after I have spoken to Dr Rachel Allen. I feel a sudden excitement at even the slight possibility of getting my life back again. I was thinking even some hypnotherapy may work to unlock my mind. I think I'd give anything a shot right now.

I think I'll try and write a complete appraisal of my time at Doncaster to see if it holds any clues as to how I might best overcome my condition. I'll keep reading that book on recovery from cults, and who knows I may even get some semblance of a life back. Wouldn't it be grand it appreciate the beauty of summers day again without having to worry about how the strong sunlight is affecting me. I can only hope that things work out alright from here. I'm hopeful that they will. I haven't felt that excitement about anything in such a long time that I don't think I would know what to do if I suddenly found myself back in possession of my emotions. I've been through so much because of my time at Doncaster that I hardly know what to do with myself. I feel as if I've lived two lives already. Ah, wouldn't it be a treat to read philosophy and write poetry again. To apply my mind to something in a constructive manner again. It almost seems to good to ever be true.

Well I think I've lost some of my ability to think. It isn't enough that I've lost those heightened thought process, but now my everyday thought process is impaired. It seems as if all I did was walk onto the cold flaw in the morning without any socks on, and wham, I lose some of my thinking capacity. This nightmare of a life just continues on, unrelenting. There's not a day which goes by that I did not lose a part of myself. Though at times I feel so close to being my old self again. Oh what a joy it would be if this condition was just some sort of brain washing that one day would just disappear. I would have all my old interests and loves back, my great ambitions and plans. No that's not true, I never was all that ambitious. All I wanted to do was lead a spiritual life, which was cruelly taken away from me.

I still don't know what I'm going to do with myself. The only thing which really appealed to me was to become a philosophy lecturer. Maybe I could one day open up a bookstore. One things for sure, I'll have to overcome this horrible situation to get my life going in some direction. For at the moment all I can do is live from one day to the next, not even dreaming of hope, just living. But to have a fulfilled life you must do more than just survive. But this situation is at times so debilitating that I know not what to do. Everyone needs dreams and ambitions. I guess one of my short term dreams is to be able to complete my honours year. There are times when I think it almost impossible. But if somehow I can overcome this situation then its something I would dearly love to do. I'll see how I go in my last assignment before I make any decisions.

Writing has always been a love and I hope someday to recapture the sharpness of mind to be really able to write with a passion again. See that's the thing, I now lack passion in the things that I do, and I was the sort of person who always followed his passion. In fact I could never really do anything that I didn't have a passion for. How do I run my life without passion? That is one thing that Robert Blackburn has done to me - short circuit my passion and conviction. Something which has in effect crippled me. How can a person such as myself live without the guidance of passion? At times it makes life unbearable. I guess passion and emotion are complimentary things, and to lose emotion means to loose passion, which I guess is what's happened to me. The only thing I could possibly have a passion for is writing. Sitting down of an evening to write these few notes is the only thing which gives me pleasure. It takes me back to a time when life held so much promise.

Another thing that I must mention that makes my life a living hell are the elastic band type strings which seem to attach themselves to me when I sometimes leave my bedroom. They seem to grasp at the very fibres of my being, even somehow stretching my mind. It is quite an uncomfortable experience and reduces my perceptions to the level of something like a homeless person. There seems no explanation for this strange occurrence - except that perhaps they have something to do with agoraphobia - fear of leaving the house. I tend to disagree with this interpretation, for when these strings take hold I am in no fear of leaving the house at all, in fact quite the opposite. I'm usually wanting very much to leave the house and go to do what I am doing. It's quite frustrating because it ruins my mind (yet another thing). It seems to only happen when I think about the strings just before I leave my room. And it only happens when I'm thinking about them. The damage usually heals itself by the next day, but it is still a very uncomfortable experience. I wonder what in the world could be causing them. I have to just remember through all of this that there is nothing physically wrong with my mind. These intrusions into my consciousness are only temporary. I will still be able to write and think. It's very hard to describe just how all these things affect my thinking capacity. I say that they reduce them, but at the end of the day I am still able to think, it's just somehow on a different level. These strings affect the very fibre of my being somehow, not allowing me to fully appreciate my surroundings. I remember once taking a walk on a beautiful autumn day, and these strings were affecting me so I couldn't even appreciate the day at all. The sky was so golden red, it normally would have exhilarated me, but this time it failed to move me, simply because of these strings and their effect. For someone like me they are intolerable. I try to fight against them, but there just too powerful. They affect me just too much.

Diary of a Schizophrenic

After just having visited the art gallery I now know just how decimated my life has become. I can no longer appreciate the great works of art with the same intensity as I used to. There's just an empty vacuity where that faculty used to be. I think I was born to appreciate the finer things of life, but now all I can do is survive. It's so frustrating to be so close to all those things you once love, but now cannot. I still buy the great texts and listen to the great music almost out of habit. There is just no appreciation there anymore. All I have is my memories of a time when things weren't so lost. When the world was full of promise and delight. I think I was destined for great things, but perhaps just a little too intense. Can that be a failing? I think in my case it was. Oh, to be able to look on the great works of art again with the same intensity, the same joy and delight. I think I would give anything. It's not enough that I once tasted such things, in fact it makes it all the more worse. My life has come to a complete standstill. There is almost nothing to go on for. But no, I go on with memory of what I once was, and perhaps still with the joy of writing to guide me I can go on living. I guess no one has to know what a mess my insides has become. They can still think I was the man I was. But in the end that doesn't matter too much, for I know, and the knowledge makes life hard to live. To have had something and lost it is the greatest crime. To have felt the greatest emotions that a human can, and then to feel them no more is a travesty of the largest proportions. I can still remember when I was just emerging into these wonderful things. Ah, what a time of joy. They were the days I guess some would say. This must be how someone feels once he has reached the end of days. The difference being that that person has a whole lifetime which to look back upon, not just a few months. I hope I never forget what I should have been. I hope I can live with those memories forever - for memories are all I have. Some say that people must learn to live in the face of such adversity, but I'd guess these people have never experienced life as I have. To be earmarked as someone great and have your life cruelly dashed is something very hard to live by. Not that I was ever going to be really great, but someone special at least. This may sound somewhat conceited but I believe it to be the truth. I think that's how all my troubles started, I couldn't just let my life go once it was over. I had to still fight for those grand things. For life for me was meant to be lived in the grandest style. There was never going to be a humdrum life for me (though now I do indeed live one).

I guess I can still live life under the pretence of what it was going to become. This sounds somewhat strange, but I believe I can still somehow do it. I can still write, I can still listen I can still see, and even though the same intensity is no longer there, perhaps I can fake it - fake it to myself. This sound like something very strange to do, but I think it's the only thing which I can do to keep on living. I can't just lead an ordinary life, I wasn't born for it. I have to somehow just pretend that nothing has happened and go on living. I guess its something of a lie to live that way, but how else can I live. When my passion and intensity has just dried up, how can I go on living just a sterile and almost non-existent life? There seemed no point. I've always been creative and I feel that I still am able to write, so I still have two of the ingredients for a full life. These however seem the only ingredients - and I has it a guess that my creativity has been handed something of a battering after the loss of my emotions. Gee that sounds strange even writing such sentiments. How does one just lose their emotion? Well it's happened and I can still hardly believe it.

I now know the one thing in the world which I would dearly love to be. An intellectual. But do I still have the mental functioning to achieve such a goal. I have to say, Robert Blackburn was right in trying to push me down the scholarship road. It's a path I would have enjoyed immensely. To sit around all day thinking and writing articles would have been a joy. Ah! I've caught myself writing in the past tense. But at the moment it seems so tragically so. Even with the help I'm getting, there are just to many setbacks to the functioning of my mind. To many things

Diary of a Schizophrenic

affect its functioning capacity. It felt like I had finally lost my mind yesterday but simply looking at the cat while I was reading a book on Rembrandt. And also, because my desires and passion are so insipidly weak at the moment I find it hard to really get motivated. I still find myself buying books in the past tense - that is buying them under the pretence that I would have enjoyed them in the past. All the classics which I love seem so far out of reach. I love the idea of reading them, but for more poor embattled mind they seem too much. I bought Homer's *Odyssey* today, and could only think while I was reading it how great it would have been to read a year ago. I think Robert Blackburn was definitely right about the sort of lifestyle I would have like to have had. But am I just saying that now when I perceive my life to be over. No I don't think so. Although at the time I had other idea's I guess I was wrong. Scholarship was and is definitely for me. Despite everything that's happened to me I still have the ability to write and it gives me a great joy. I just wishing I had had that love a year ago, and stuck buy it. It would have given my life a lot more focus and direction. I can't believe I went of on such a tangent. It was the intellectual life that was always going to give me the greatest happiness. But is it too late? As I said before, all I can do is lead my life as if it still was like it was. Just try and imagine I still have the same feelings and perceptions that I did before all this came upon me. It still isn't a bad life under such pretence. I guess just having started to read the life story of T. S. Eliot, it makes me realise just what my life could have been. I could have been leading a similar life. I became too short sighted in my outlook a year ago, and it has cost me dearly. Oh, how I wish I had that time all over again, there would be so many things I would have done differently. I guess hindsight is a wonderful thing.

I think it's all finally become too hard. I've just gotten too low. I just got out of a chair and it felt as if I'd left my whole soul behind. Even writing these few word has become something of a chore. I can't pretend to be well when there is virtually nothing left inside. There is literally nothing left of me. I feel as if I'm nothing but a walking zombie. It such a shame because I was feeling like I could finally cope with what was going on. But as usual something hits me right at the very end to bring me back down. I just can't pretend anymore, Oh it's too much, this is definitely a fate worse than death. To have experienced the wonderful gifts which I once did and to have them taken away is too much to bear. There seems no way out, no escape. Listening to music has become nothing more than a blank experience. There isn't even the memory of what it used to be like. But that's just like so many other facets of my life. I was born for greater heights, not to be cast down within these confines. I guess I can do nothing but mope around the house.

I once had quite an exhilarating imagination. I could imagine almost all the places that I'd been in great detail. But like so much of my life, my imagination has deserted me. To live the life of imagination is one of the greatest gifts a person can have. It frees your soul to explore new ground. Not to mention allowing a person to enjoy the fruits of reading poetry. That's one of things that's become so hard, is to read poetry and hear the poet talk of the beauties of the natural world, and to know that I will never again appreciate such things. I don't think I could have written a script more precise if I was trying to imagine the worst possible scenario for my life to go. It seems almost uncanny.

It's almost seems too nightmarish to be true. I think I've just lost the mind that perceives a joy in books. I just caught a glimpse of bookshelf as I was walking past it and then I happened to look outside and there was a glaring light. It pierced my mind and shattered I guess the mind which I had activated. I just can't believe it. I now look at my bookshelf and there's this horrible blank looking back at me, whether there used to be a fine appreciation of books. I hope it hasn't also affect the joy I get from writing, but I have a horrible feeling that it has. I was just starting really enjoy my scholarship again and this has to happen. It seems too horrible to be true. The only thing which I have to enjoy in my life has been taken away, just like that. What an

Diary of a Schizophrenic

absolutely meaningless existence I must now endure. I hope my mind can somehow endure and regenerate itself. For I don't know if I could go on if this is to be my lot in life. With no enjoyment of writing my life ceases to hold meaning. There is then nothing left for me to live for. I was just starting to really enjoy myself spending the day typing away and the nights relaxing. I really felt I was once again loving, which I something which I haven't done in such a long time. It seems so unfair that it should be taken away from me just now. I only live in hope that it can rejuvenate itself. I know there's nothing physiologically wrong with my mind so it should be able to right itself over time. But I'm sick of waiting. It seems my entire life is spent waiting for my mind to heal itself. I spend the large portion of my life walking around with a broken mind. Oh cruelty. To show me the delight of books and then to snatch it away.

I hope and pray that I haven't lost my scholarly minds. The joy that I've recently acquired for writing can't have left me now, though I fear it has. Robert Blackburn foretold that I would lose my scholarship, and it seems as if his prediction has come true. I never realised just how accurate his prediction has been. It's just a matter of hoping now that I can somehow get my scholarly mind back. There is hope still.

Have I lost the ability to write? Is it gone never to return? I guess I'll find out tomorrow when I attempt to continue work on my essay. How could this happen write now, as I'm just about to complete my B A. If my life wasn't a nightmare before, it is now. Although I think I've had the seeds planted in my mind to continue on with my studies. I would dearly love to complete my honours year, and I need all my best minds to achieve it. I can't just go into with the blank mind which I have now. Oh please don't let it be so. I'm not getting the enjoyment from this writing as I have been in the past. By ability to write is my life, please don't take it away from me. It would absolutely kill me. There would cease to be any reason to keep on living. I've already lost my ability to appreciate beauty, and artwork, please don't let me lose my ability to write, it's all I have in the world. There's nothing I enjoy more. I guess I'm still writing this so there's still hope, but somehow it isn't the same, there's now joy to it. It just is a blank is. Oh Pleeeeeeeaase, don't let me lose this. To have lost my emotion was bad enough, but not this, it's taking too much from somebody. What did Tillyard say about the tragic?

I'm just wanting to write few things to convince myself that I can still write. Ah good, I can at least feel some enjoyment as I write. I thought for a second there that the ability and the enjoyment had left me. There's been so much that I've lost that I wasn't sure if writing was yet another thing. It seems as if I have a fatalistic mind which will convince itself of the worst. It still doesn't feel completely right, but I'm sure that will just come with time. I've really enjoyed exercising my literary talents on this last assignment. Writing on a laptop has indeed been a joy. I think if I had have had a laptop a year ago it would have saved me a lot of misguided adventures. And not to mention a lot of heartache. Ah that's better, I can feel the flow starting to course through my mind. Its something I truly hope I never lose is the ability to write. I'll have to augment my skills by reading something like *The Kings English* - a book I should have read a long time ago. I can't believe how misguided my life had become. I had totally lost direction on some fool hardy quest. Music, art, reading and writing should have always been my primary concerns. To have stuck to those basics would have saved myself a lot of time and trouble. I'm still living with the after effects of my little foray into the realms of spiritual awakening. Someday I will finally come to terms with what's happened to me. It will be a long and windy road, but I believe it can be travelled - nay I must travel it for my life to continue. Well it seems to be continuing anyway, sometimes with me kicking and screaming. I'll finally have my day though, when my mind is right and there's nothing left to do but study and write. Who knows maybe someday I will write my life story. With some help I'm sure its possible. I think it would be quite an interesting story if I could remember half of it. The journey of the mind is perhaps the most terrifying journey to take, and I took the ride of a lifetime.

Well I think it's finally happened, I've lost the ability to write academic pieces. I know I'm now writing, but its something of a different matter to write a scholarly article. Robert Blackburn once warned me that I would lose scholarship, and I guess it's finally happened. What sort of life am I to lead now? Something also happened to my consciousness last night. It feels like the catheda tube on a TV when it blows out, my consciousness just suddenly got smaller. It's hard to describe but it's as if my consciousness just got smaller - and as a result I've lost the imaginative faculty of my mind. It was just starting to come along, I was creating some very striking visualisations. But like so much of my life it is now gone to. And because of what happened to my consciousness I'm not getting the same pleasure out of writing this. It's as if somehow the keyboard has gotten smaller in a very weird sort of way. How can I contemplate a life without writing, or for that matter reading? Now that's something that hasn't left me yet. I can still read in short burst. In fact I was quite enjoying reading T. S. Eliot's biography. I see a lot of parallels in his early life to that of mine. Except he went on to lead a life that I can no longer dream of. Without the ability to write my life has come to standstill. Well I guess I can give it one more day before I close the book for good on my writing. I can't believe it, all I did was look at my bookshelf and then out the window and I was blinded by a glancing ray of light, and wham, my ability to write has just left me. I guess this has been my fate every since I left Doncaster. Robert Blackburn has been eerily correct in his predictions. I never thought he could be so correct. But what does this mean for the rest of my life. It doesn't paint a rosy picture. There doesn't seem much left to do but hope and pray - hope that I can somehow get my writing skills back. They left me along with my appreciation for books. I used to be able to look at books and get quite a sense of satisfaction, just by looking at them. But along with my ability to appreciate art that sense of appreciation has left me to. I guess they must have been related. Although my ability to appreciate beauty has been gone for some time now, and I've only just lost my ability to write, so I guess the two can't be related. Wow, listen to me I'm analysing this like it was a maths problem - very dry indeed.

Well all I can do is hope. That's all I've got left, and even that has in recent times deserted me. I lead nothing but a shell of an existence, I am unmoved by all that is good in the world. I fear one day I shall finally lose my mind for good. With all the intrusions into my mind it's a scary possibility. Everyday is such a roller-coaster, I never know when a ray of light is going to glance into my mind, or when a sudden turn is going to release a portion of my being.

And the trumpet sounds
For those who have bled
And those who have died
A thousand deaths a day

And we see around us
The wonderful stillness
As it breeds a certain solace
Only to be dashed
Upon an unguarded reef
Leaving us stranded
With no port to call
And no sounds to whisper
Of our own immortality
Shattered beneath a June sea

And the sounds are those
Of the beholden waste
which we have now forgotten
Or forgiven
Whichever suits our daily mood

And we love to linger
Just to sample briefly
Of the sweet magnanimity
That was yours to offer
To that chosen few

Diary of a Schizophrenic

Who now stand unguarded
unrepentant
upon a chanceless breeze

That's it, I've lost the ability to think critically, and more importantly the ability to write scholarly material has left me. Robert Blackburn was right. All I did was look at my bookshelf and then out the window and the light seared my brain. And just to compound things I was lying in bed this morning and I just felt some of my soul just leave me, just like that. I now feel like I did when I was a teenager. I've regressed back to that point in my life. I've lost my heart as well as my writing ability. I can't believe this has happened to me just before I was due to complete my B A. I don't know how I'm going to pass my final exam when I can't even think critically anymore. This life has treated me disastrously. They let me have the greatest gifts that a man can posses and then, to have them stripped away, is a fate no one should go through. All I want to do is to be a scholar, but it now looks like I won't get the chance. I should have stayed at Doncaster where I was being encouraged to take that path. I look at my life now and it seems worthless. No beauty, no emotion, and now no writing, coupled with a loss of heart. There seems no end to the torment which I am forced to undergo. Oh when will it end? When will I finally get what I want? I fear it's out of my grasp now, baring some sort of miracle. All I want to do is be a scholar. How much is that to ask? I guess not everyone gets to be one. The intellectual life would have suited me just fine. If only I had gone to Doncaster that day a year ago. I could hear a voice inside me telling me to go, but instead I went to the philosophy library and ruined my mind by reading. I now regret having left Doncaster. Robert Blackburn offered me a life very few get to sample. Oh, now I can't even write and I feel like I did when I was a teenager. There's just no motivation in me anymore. Oh cruel fate. How does this happen to someone? It seems to nightmarish to be true. All I can do is go on now, with no hope and no joy, and no scholarship which is the worst thing that could have befallen me. To lose that part of myself that can study just decimates my life. There is no point to life. Just a life of mere existence, with no intellectual ability whatsoever. I feel like its the end, I can see no way out. And this has all happened just before I am about to complete my B A. I guess this means I won't be doing honours. Why can I write like this and not in an intellectual vein? It seems an impossibility.

Well I think its well and truly official, I've lost the ability to write. If I didn't have to contend with enough in my life, I lose the one thing I am gifted at. Its comparable to Beethoven going deaf - well no its isn't because he could still write music. I just don't know what to do with myself. After getting this laptop I was finally starting to enjoy writing again, but I guess it was only a matter of time before that pleasure was also denied me. It seems strange to say, but having lost my abilities as a scholar it has impacted in all other areas of my life. I still enjoy books, but it just isn't the same any more. My appreciation of music has also been affected. It's as if they were all tied into the same part of my mind which was destroyed. There's simply nothing left for me to enjoy. I can't enjoy movies because of the loss of my emotions, I can't enjoy art because of the loss of my appreciation of beauty, I can't enjoy books with the same intensity because I've lost the ability to write, and I can't enjoy music for the same reason. Talk about a person's life being brought to its knees. All I have is my frustration, and even that is getting somewhat tiresome. I wonder what I've got left to do with my life. The only thing I can think of is to get a job in a bookstore, but with the current state of my mind that seems an impossibility. I'll just keep plodding along day after day, letting this nightmare of a life take its toll. I guess the one positive is that I'm not dying of some degenerative brain disease like I thought I was. There is simply nothing left to enjoy. And I'm a man who does things with passion, or I guess I did things with passion - past tense. There is no passion left in me. No that's not true, I have a passion to write, but that's just a torture now that I've lost that ability. I can't believe all this has happened just before my final exam.

Diary of a Schizophrenic

Its only one exam to go before the end of my B A and I lose the ability to write and think critically. You can't deny it's a nightmare. I guess I can almost laugh at the way my life has turned out. It could hardly be any worse. At least I still have my body in tacked - that's something I guess. And what makes it all infinitely worse is that I can feel no emotion about it whatsoever. There's no sorrow about what's going on, just a cold emotional blank. And me, with some of the intense emotions possible. I guess all I can do is live - no not live, survive.

Well the trials and traumas of my life continue. Would you believe that now I've lost the ability to gain pleasure from books, perhaps the one last thing that gave me pleasure. I could look at them, and get a feeling from them. It reminded of time when I could have been a scholar. It was quite a nice feeling. But now like so much of my life, that ability has left me also. I was only looking forward to some nice relaxation after my final exam when I walked into a stray ray of light, and wham my mind went. It's amazing how light can sear your mind. Its a condition that is very hard to imagine, but is sufficient to make my life a living hell. This is after I felt at last some respite from my existence last night. I was listening to program on Beethoven and was quite enjoying listening to how he wrote his music. It mode me long for the time when I could write and the creative process that goes on when you write. But as usual something intervened to ruin my respite. I just sat back in my chair and felt the creaking sound it made run up my back. The new mindset I had just achieved was immediately destroyed, and I couldn't appreciate the program as I had been. There's not a day which goes by in which I do not lose a part of myself somehow. Now that my final pleasure has been taken away from me I'm at a loss as to what to do. If I couldn't be a scholar, I could always fantasise about being a scholar. I can't even do that anymore. I guess I'll continue to buy books, just in remembrance of what I used to be. Though I have to admit to myself that it's finally over. Without my love affair with books, without my writing, without my appreciation of the arts and of music, I have nothing. It has been successively taken away from me, all of it. How does one live? How does one continue on? I wasn't born to lead the senseless existence which I now face, my destiny was for greater things. I can't think of one thing that now gives me any pleasure, not to mention any sense of worth-whileness. I can't even feel depressed at my plight, for I can no longer feel emotions. This last attack on my consciousness has really done some damage. I can't even see the world in the half way that I did before. There's just this animal-like existence. I had to read John Stuart Mill on Utilitarianism for my last essay, and it was interesting him talking of the higher and the lower pleasures, and how a person who can enjoy the higher pleasures would never trade them for the lower ones. It seems as if I've totally lost the ability to appreciate the higher pleasures, and according to Mill that's what gives a life its happiness. Better to be Socrates dissatisfied than a pig satisfied. Well I've gone from being the Dissatisfied Socrates to the less than satisfied pig. Well that's what it seems like at any rate. All I can do now is pretend like I enjoy the higher pleasures. I can go to the art gallery and look at my favourite 16th and 17th century Italian masters, and just pretend like I can still appreciate them - or maybe remember what it was like when I did appreciate them. I can turn on the radio and pretend like I'm enjoying what I hear. But there's no one there to watch me, I'm only pretending to myself. I'm fooling no one but myself. But a person has to have a life. There has to be interests and things to motivate a person. There can't just be a blank nothing. Well in my case unfortunately there is nothing but a blank nothing. So I must pretend, pretend to lead the life I was going to. Reading writing, poetry, art, music - these are the things I loved. These are the things which I must continue to see at least some grain of pleasure - if not that then just the remembrance, the joy of remembering what I could have been. Ah, if only I could go back to my youthful self and tell him how to do things properly. I would be leading quite a wonderful life. It just seems so far away now.

Diary of a Schizophrenic

When I think about it, I really could have been a great philosopher lecturer. The insights that I used to have into some of the philosophical texts were quite deep. The more time which I have to spend going over the past, the more I realise just what I missed. I would really have loved to have been a scholar. The hours of writing and research would have suited me just fine. I can only say that I let a perfect opportunity pass me by. My life now just doesn't allow me to write like I once did. I can't think in the same fashion that I once did. Philosophy seems unable to move me, although most everything is unable to move me. The joy I used to get out of reading philosophers such as Wittgenstein and Derrida has deserted me. Oh, why can't I write again? To write and think, what noble pursuits, things which I used to do with great intensity. Even writing this just make me realise what a joy the writing life would have been. To really learn the use of words - all the terminology and the usage of words; it could have been a life long journey, the journey through words. That's all I need, is to have an intellectual project going, like I did with my studies into the philosophy of language. That was my little baby. I could really have had a good time researching and studying everything there has to do with language. I definitely would have written my honours thesis on the topic. But honours now seems so far away. It's something that I really want to do. To have gone on and done a PHD would have been a great pleasure. But it now seems like I won't get the chance. All I need is my ability to write back again, and everything will be alright. But I can't have it back. Maybe one day that part of my mind that was destroyed will make a come back and I'll be able to write again. Because there really is nothing like the feeling of writing. To gain a great insight into the workings of some philosopher, and to write those insights down is quite an exhilarating feeling. There has to be someway to recapture that. But I think it somehow beyond me now. All I have are the memories of what it was like - and what I could have been. I guess in a way its those memories which keep me going.

I can't believe how drastically just patting the cat affects my mind. Its difficult to describe just what happens, but its like there's just a big brick wall being erected within my mind, baring me from experiencing some of the qualities of my mind. It's so frustrating. It affected my imagination, my memory, my ability formulate words, basically my whole perception is affected. How is this possible? Is there some agent which shoots up my arm when I'm stroking the cat, which enters directly into my mind? But that's just an impossibility. What could it possibly be then? I'm afraid of talking to anyone about it for fear they may think me odd. There's just no explanation for this phenomenon, but it makes my life hell. I guess the only solution is not to pat the cat, but she seems one of my only friends at the minute. And it seems a very temperamental occurrence. Sometimes it affects me more than others, just this time it has perhaps affected me the most drastically. I think this whole situation I am suffering through is all related. Somehow something happened to my mind to open it up, and its now at the mercy of the elements. There are just a whole lot of factors which affect it. There's not a day goes by where I don't get drastically affected by something. I had just finally decided to live my life the way it should have been when this happened. It's so frustrating. It seems whenever I begin to even think about enjoying something it gets taken away. I don't ask for much, but I guess I'll never get what I want. All I want is to be able to appreciate things again - art, music, nature, literature, philosophy. Just to have my old life back basically. I guess I'm just too susceptible to my environment to ever have any chance of leading the life that I want to. I can't even begin to imagine what a happy and contented life must feel like. No I never really wanted just happiness, only to live and work in what I loved to do. That's all I ask. Is that too much? For the time being I believe it must be. And I think of what I could of been, and then I think of what I am now, and it makes me sad. I feel no better than a rock at times, with what's happened to me that's just the way I feel. I guess there's no respite for me. Nothing to give any pleasure. All I want to do is to be a scholar. I guess I had the chance.

Diary of a Schizophrenic

I think the only thing left to do is to lead my life the way it was supposed to be led. I would have been an intellectual, so from now on I'm going to lead my life as if I still can follow that dream. It means going to the theatre, to concerts, to poetry readings. It means reading all the great texts and writing about them - writing down what I think about them. Although I've lost my capacities as critical thinker, I believe this is still possible for me. I might even go down to the city baths once a week for a swim. I'll also do some travelling, perhaps to London and Paris, exploring all the art galleries and bookstores. It's a life that I should have started to lead a long time ago. I can't remain stuck in this sterile world any longer. If I'm still alive I have to start living, no matter what the cost. I have a feeling that it won't be as traumatic as I expect it to be. I'll just have to pretend that I've still got all my appreciations for these things. I just simply can't go on with life the way it is going. There's nothing to live for. With nothing to move me there seems little point doing the external things, but I must try. At least trying will give me some relief from this hell of a world I'm inhabiting. This sterile existence is not going to get the better of me. I just hope doing things like going to the theatre and to concerts won't affect me too much. It would be quite a shame if I couldn't sit through a performance. But I must at least try. Try and do something to raise the quality of my existence. I'll continue to write my little diary entries and listen to music. I'd also love to do a study of some of William Blake's work, but I don't feel myself capable anymore. I've just lost my critical faculties. To spend the next six months doing my own private studies would be quite a treat - I hope there's some way I can possibly do it. I just hope my mind is up to the task. I keep forgetting that I've got a whole life ahead of me, and there's something I've got to do to occupy my time. And no just occupy, but occupy meaningfully - if anything can be meaningful to my life at the moment.

When I think about what I could have become it makes me quite frustrated. I could have really contributed something to the world. I had a great ability to write and appreciate things. I had a heightened sensitivity to all things religious. It could have been quite a worthwhile life. But I compare it to the life which I lead now and all I can do is sigh. There's no life left anymore, just frustrating aspirations which can no longer be fulfilled. I hate to keep writing these journey entries like my life is already over, but it just seems so overwhelmingly the case. I guess the most positive I've been is talk of pretending to live my life the way it should have been lead. But I tried by going to theatre and I just couldn't appreciate it. It was just a deadening experience. There was no enjoyment whatsoever. I just hate to think what the rest of my life has in stall for me. I guess I could be contented with my life if I just had the simple things in my life. I can't even see the future anymore, I literally can't see it - its just not there. You know that feeling in your gut when you look forward to something coming up, well I haven't felt that for too long. Even the enjoyment for a cup of tea has left me. There's just no enjoyment of anything. My life has gotten into this bland routine in which I can see my life just zipping by. It doesn't really matter how fast it goes, because I'm not really that concerned with holding onto any of it - There's nothing left to hold on to. All I can do is remember what things were like, or perhaps what they were going to be like. I guess tragedy happens everyday in life, and I just happen to be just another tragedy. Why can't I even feel depressed at the thought of that? There's just so much in my life that's going wrong that I find it hard to believe at times. Reading the biography of T. S. Eliot has really opened my eyes to what my life could have become. I could have studied overseas, got a PHD and been quite comfortable being a man of intellectual prowess. I had the talent, and its so frustrating to know that in the face of the life which I now lead.

I ache for the intellectual life. It's where I should be. I still get glimpses in my mind of what it would have been like. It would have been a great life. There would have been

Diary of a Schizophrenic

nothing better than taking my laptop to country cottages and writing great philosophical treatises. I had the ability to be quite a good writer. I can't believe the opportunity has passed me by. All I can do is live a parallel life. To do the things I should have done. But there's no joy left in them anymore. It's all just dried up. I remember hearing a young man and women having a philosophical conversation in the Gibson Library when I was studying for an exam. It really struck home, because I realised I will never be able to have a conversation like that ever again. Those sort of things were my life blood. They gave my life its meaning - and now they are no more. There's a world out there which I just am unable to participate in anymore, the intellectual life. University life is where I should be. I should be involved in all the societies and clubs, listening to people give papers at the various philosophical societies, basically being involved. But all that is beyond me now. I only had a very short taste of what that was like about a year and a half ago now. I really felt as if I finally belonged. It was a life that really appealed to me. It's so frustrating to have such memories in the face of what I now am. I sometimes feel as if I could go on and study, but those moments are very few and far between. My mind is simply not what it used to be. How can a person go from being what I was to what I am now? It seems a tragic impossibility. Another thing which is really frustrating is to read the T. S. Eliot biography and realise what parallels in life we had. It shows me just what I could have become. I guess one day I will somehow come to terms with what's happened to my life, but I have a sneaking suspicion that I never will. What has happened has been to debilitating. What I want from life I can no longer have. I've always been one to follow my passions and when I can't it seems as if there is no more life left to live.

I hope I haven't lost my cat. She's not back home yet and it's quite late. It's very unlike her to be away for any length of time. I just have this really bad feeling that something has happened to her. That would just be absolutely devastating. She is perhaps the one thing that gives my life any pleasure, the one thing that I have in my life. I know that sounds funny of a cat, but I'm afraid its true. I have no friends, I have no inner life, the only thing I have is a cat. I just hope she's alright somewhere. I couldn't believe it if she was gone. There would just be an empty void in my life. I don't know what I would do with myself.

Oh how I wish I had my intellectual capacities working again. I know I sound something like a broken record, always harping about how I would have loved to have been an intellectual – it's just that it is so true. That's exactly where what's left of my heart lies. To be an intellectual, a philosopher lecturer would be a joy incomparable. While I'm reading this autobiography of T. S. Eliot I keep remembering what my life was like and how it could have turned out. I think what I'm doing is substituting writing about my longings for the intellectual life for my inabilities to use my intellectual faculties anymore - yes that seems to be it. I now almost forget what it was like having all those wonderful insights into the mind of Wittgenstein and the like. It was the philosophy of language which was my little baby. I had a wonderful relationship with that branch of philosophy. I seemed to understand it quite well. How did I lose that? I guess it was a long list of occurrences which happened to me that long year ago. I don't think I'll ever fully understand what happened to me. At any rate it's not something that should happen to anybody. To lose those faculties after you've had them is a travesty. Something I would not wish on anybody. I guess I can still reason these philosophers, but it just isn't the same. It's very hard to describe exactly what's happened, but there seems to be a general lack of insight and critical responsiveness into these philosophers. There's simply no appreciation there anymore for these things. Like much of my life it is the appreciation which has gone. How does one lose an appreciation of things? Well I seemed to be the model for just that sort of loss. I guess it's that experience with the sight which has the most dramatic affect on my mind. Maybe it has something to do with that. Or maybe it's just a horrible nightmare that I will one day wake up from. Wake up to find all my sensibilities fully interacted, just ready for me to resume the life I should be leading. I also miss my religious sensibilities. I guess that's what I was essentially, a religious person. Gee what sort of a life am I left with? One in which I simply live from one day to the next. Not expecting anything from life whatsoever.

Well it's happened, I've lost the ability to appreciate art. I decided to go to the National Gallery of Victoria this afternoon to see a new exhibition which is on there. It's an exhibition of 17th and 18th century American and Australian landscape painting. Now I used to have quite a love of landscape painting, but today there was no response from me at all. It was quite an unnerving experience. I would look at the paintings and get very little response at all. I used to love just to look and imagine as if I was really there, but even that was denied me. I guess losing your emotional faculty has quite an impact upon one's ability to appreciate art. But there was hardly any response whatsoever! Just perhaps a few odd memories of what it was like when I could appreciate such things. It seems as if I am nothing more than a shell of my former self. And my inability to appreciate is not restricted simply to landscape art. I was in the gallery bookstore, which usually inspires me to pine for days gone by, but this time there was just no response from the art I was seeing. I picked up a book on Rembrandt, who I used to really appreciate, and there was nothing, no response again. I was getting quite concerned. It isn't enough to live the sterile existence that I live, but to have my love of art taken away is quite a travesty. It was quite a sterile feeling, not being able to be moved by what I saw. I guess I should have been warned, for the art on the walls in my room also fails to move me now. I remember being quite taken by William Blake's painting "Pity" which I have in my room, but it also now fails to move me. I guess I should cease to be surprised by such occurrences now, after all I have been through, but I seem to be unable to cope with it. I mean how could you with the total decimation of the inner world. To have been given the gifts which I had been and then to have them taken away is something I'm afraid I will never get used to. My life was art, music, religion reading and writing. Well at least I seem to still be able to read. There have been times when even that has deserted me, but at least it comes back. Once again I ask myself, "how is one to live?" And again I answer, simply day by day, there is no their way to live. Each day will bring its own trials and tribulations, but hopefully its own respites from this intolerable world. I must somehow go on. In the face of my overwhelming loss I must somehow find the strength to continue.

I couldn't believe it, yesterday my ability to write returned. It was quite a joyous feeling, I almost found out to hard to believe. I was swimming in a wonderful sea of words. Great long and complex sentences were just flying out of my mind in a fantastic avalanche of literary joy. It was a symphony of incredibly intense wordsmanship. I found it difficult to believe it could be happening again. My mind was simply racing. Although it of course all cam crashing to a horrible end. As I was pacing backwards and forwards, just marvelling at the wonders my mind was producing, when all of a sudden my mind jumped out of my body and attached itself to the cat. What a horrible experience. It was like a great long elastic band of an effect, that shot straight out of my head and onto the cat. I couldn't escape it, no matter where I walked to in the house, it just kept on being attached. I was at a loss to know what to do. And as a result the wonderful cavalcade of words came to an abrupt halt. I couldn't believe it. I finally had my life back and then it was hurriedly whisked away again. It was an awful experience that is very hard to put into words. It left me stunned and unable to properly think. Not only did it affect my mind, but my whole being as well. It ripped me apart. And it all happened just as I had started getting my mind back. There simply is no justice in this world. I guess I had something a fatalistic foreknowledge that it was too good to last and that it would come tumbling down again. But I can't get over the fact that it came back again. I wish my mind was more stable, I could have certainly have a wonderful life with that sort of "word action" happening in my mind. All I could do is sit around and write. But this is all speculation

Diary of a Schizophrenic

now, for it's gone and who knows if it will come back. I'm hoping that it does, for I feel I was put on this earth to write. It is the only love left to me now. But how does one write when experience has dried up. All I can do is write of the horror which every day of my life brings. I guess that's something. Oh, I hope that writing is still there, I hope it really hasn't left again. My life is filled with enough tragedy as it is. Ah, one day I will be free.

I still pine for those long gone days were this horrible affliction did not exert its sinister power over me. I keep thinking of what my life could have become, but I think more importantly I would have been happy for my life to go nowhere, if only I hadn't lost all my appreciate faculties. To have written a PHD would have been nice, but there really was little in philosophy, apart from the philosophy of language, which interested me. It was philosophy of religion that had really captured my imagination, and I remember looking up the university directories and finding a course on religious philosophy at the ANU, and deciding that that was what I was going to do. I would have contented myself with that I think. To be a university intellectual was far from my concerns, although with my studies in religion I well may have ended up there anyway. I only wish I still had the ability to write for university, well I think I might still, after yesterdays surprising rejuvenation of my critical faculties, although today that feel like a long way away. The cat is still torturing me. I have no idea how my mind can do the things which it is doing. I only hope that its some outlandish nightmare, and that my life will return to normal at some time in the near future. Well I'm considering taking this notepad computer with me when I leave for Sydney. It should be fun to sit in the state library there and jot down some thoughts. It would have been great to have written a book at some stage in my life, I think that's what I was born to achieve. I was given the gift of writing to write a book. Sitting alone with my thoughts and a keyboard would have been quite a good life, but I guess I won't get the chance. It's such a shame because even now I can still glean some pleasure from taping away at the keyboard, even though all my other sensibilities have been lost or destroyed. It struck me today what lifeless existence I lead. I was a man who was affected very profoundly by a number of things, and now I'm like a rock. Well at least I can still write about it in these journal entries. One pleasure I hope not to lose.

I think I dearly would have loved to have written a book. Yes, to have written a book would have been a great joy in my life. In fact to have written a number of books. I guess one would have either been on William Blake or Ludwig Wittgenstein - two significant influences upon my life. They both impressed upon me very deeply. I guess it takes anywhere from a year to write a book. From the collating of all the material to the final execution of the finished text. I could also have written a book on some religious topic. My insights into the nature of religion were quite profound. It was the overriding passion of my life for a time there. There's something romantic about the idea of writing a book, it strikes me very deeply. Although I guess it's hard to write a book when your ability to write has left you - although I'm confident that it will one day return again. The joy of words and ideas is a joy one doesn't forget too soon. Although my stock of ideas seems to have dried up. I can remember those dewy winters morning when I would walk to university busily thinking away about how the latest Wittgenstein book that I'd read had affected me. I was so full of passion and commitment about my philosophy, it really kept me going through some troubling times. I seemed also be a troubled person, but the flood of insights that I would sometimes get would be quite exhilarating. I should stop such trip down memory lane, and concentrate more on my book writing fantasies. For to write a book I think would have suited my character rather well. I guess there were times when I thought I was going to be a monk, but I guess my real calling was for writing - Hey, I really should stop talking in the past tense. I seem to have at least some life to lead, and if

Diary of a Schizophrenic

yesterday is anything to go on then there might still be some significant work left in me yet. My honours year is going to be the test. If I can do well enough there and pass my degree with honours, them I will really have achieved something, given what I've been through. My one true passion now though is still to study. Although I wouldn't equate the word passion with anything I do these days.

I can't believe it, I started to feel my perceptions returning this morning, and once again they have been crippled. I started to feel "alive" again. All those little perceptions which I've missed over the past six months had returned. The feeling you get from a room, from the weather and the like. It had all come back to me. But of course it was too good to last. All I did was let Charlie sit on my lap, and wham, it was all gone again. Just like waking from a beautiful dream. There really is no justice in this world. I still can't believe it's gone. I was just starting to have some dreams for the future. I was starting to think about what it would be like to be living by myself, how I would set up my study, what sort of furniture I would get, what sort of prints I would be buying. I also stated toying with the idea of opening a bookstore, and how I might lay that out. You see, it was all coming back to me, but because of the cat it has all been taken away again. I guess my life is meant to be one tragic occurrence after another. There's not a day goes buy were I get some relief from this torment, only to have it whisked away again. One day I will overcome this, I'm sure. At times it seems so insurmountable that I dread to think what the future may hold. Though there are times when I can see through the haze to a brighter future - like this morning. But unfortunately those times are few and far between. It seems as if whenever I gain any respite from this malady, it immediately closes in and deals me yet another blow. I should cease to be surprised at occurrences like this morning. It just seems to happen on such a regular basis. That tragedy which is my life just keeps rolling on, unendingly. Though one day I hold out the hope that it will all work out. That my mind will cease to be affected by ever little occurrence during the day, and that I will be able to study consistently and complete my honours year. I guess that's my main aim, is to complete an honours year, and if I can go on to do further study after that. But it just seems like such a far distance now, these twin goals. All I can do is hope, hope that this curse will be lifted.

Well I'm now in Sydney, and have had another chance to regain my humanity. But once again my fragile mind has denied me my chance at normalcy. After having a wonderful dream in which I regained all my faculties, I woke to find myself enjoying some of the fruits of being a human which I hadn't experienced for quite some time. I felt "comfort" at sitting around the coffee table in front of a warm heater, and being surrounded by family. I realise now just what these last six months have taken out of me. I had ceased to be human. But of course after regaining some of my humanity, I once again lost it. Firstly, Cassandra turned on the television, which partially took away all the feelings which I was having. I still haven't worked out how the television affects me just yet. I then went for a walk to the shop to buy the paper for mum, and forgot to take my glasses. The sunlight immediately took my mind away. Another thing which is very hard to explain. I was beginning to feel my ability to write return again before the cruel blow was once more handed down upon my poor self. The tragedy which is my life just continues on its merry course. I have a feeling though that in the not too distant future I will make a full recovery. I will then be able to go on and do all the things I've dreamed about for so long. To write an honours thesis and to maybe to some further study. But most importantly I may in fact regain my humanity. It is all the little human perceptions which I have been missing. Everything that makes a person human. The joys, the sorrows, the ups the downs. It is all these things which have left me, and I began even to not notice that they had gone, so ensconced I had become in my predicament. All I dream now is to continue to have mornings such as this one to keep regenerating myself to the wonderful possibilities of humanity. It was a joy to finally have some of them back, and it will be a further

Diary of a Schizophrenic

joy to have them stay for a little bit longer next time - and then the time after that even a little bit longer. Oh I am ecstatic at the thought, well as ecstatic as I can possibly be in the state in which I'm in.

Well today was perhaps the first day in which I've felt alive for some considerable amount of time. I've been even making some quite casual observations as to the goings on of the people around me. Something I've been unable to accomplish for quite an extended period. I guess I like to think of it as my little void, a world without human experience of many kinds. But it's good to be finally seeing some relief. It's only come in the smallest of graces so far, but I'm hopeful that it will soon extend into a more profound and sustained recapturing of my human faculties. To even be thinking of the future is great step for me, one I haven't taken for too long. I'm hopeful that this very encouraging trend continues, but I guess I can only hope. Things are still affecting me quite substantially, and this infernal hypersensitivity is still plaguing my every action. I hope one day to finally overcome such a situation and lead the life I want to. Although even talking of such an eventuality is encouraging. I continue to read T. S. Eliot's biography and it continues to fascinate me. There are aspects of the man which I found in myself before all this trouble began. I hope to one day regain a semblance of that personality which I left behind, for it is indeed something which I miss dearly. I think I finally will be happy when I can once again enjoy the fineries of nature - a joy which has for too long absented itself form my daily routines. A healthy appreciation of beauty is an essentially requisite for any aspiring young man - though aspiration is another thing which I seemed to have left behind. It is now however returning to me, which is I guess something to be quite happy about. I long for the day when I can once again revel in the use of words. It's something I miss almost as much as my sense of the beautiful. Today I went hunting in a bookstore and found a book on Albert Durer and Rubens. I guess to appreciate there work again is a small blessing. I have to be thankful for these small gifts. To be human again is something which I'm quite enjoying. I've missed it for too long, although what I'm experiencing now is only a shadow what I might experience in the future. I'm very optimistic now that I can somehow fashion a life with constituent parts that I am once again given. I'm sure that having lived so long without them will mean my appreciation of them will be exceptionally heightened.

Last night I had it all back again. I was once again swimming in words. It was quite a joyous sensation. But of course it couldn't last. I was talking to someone and they began talking in quite strong terms about Diana, princess of Wales. The person obviously has a passion for the princess. Anyway, she was talking in such strong terms that she shattered my fragile mind. I couldn't believe it, I had it all back, I was writing essays in mind. The words had returned with such force that I was almost in shock as to exactly what to do. But of course it couldn't last. It was frustrating to lose it once again. I was actually starting to have my dreams again about going on the PHD standard. I was actually feeling that alive to the world of words. I was dreaming about how I was going to set up my study, in fact how I was going to set up my house. There was going to be little garden in the back for me to totter around when I needed a break from my study. I was going to have a fireplace in the study, with two bookshelves full of books. There was going to be the writing desk there for me which dad is going to buy for me. And of course my print of Blake's 'Pity' hanging over the desk. I was going to have a gentleman's reading chair in the corner with perhaps a largish window. It was going to be the perfect study environment. I was really feeling alive yesterday, for the first time in, oh, I don't remember how long. But those perceptions have now left me. It is yet another tragedy in an already tragedy filled existence. I know it wasn't the person's fault, but gee it was a painful experience watching my newly won future slipping through my fingers. I hardly know what to do with myself. I only hope I get another chance to experience the kind scholarly aspirations that I did

Diary of a Schizophrenic

yesterday again. I finally felt as if I had arrived at where I need to be going, as if my life was finally taking some shape into a form that I could at last appreciate. I just hope I haven't lost that ability to use words. It's such a joy to be in command of the English language. I was actually writing essays in my head. It was grand experience. One I hope to emulate again soon. I just hope it hasn't all left me. I guess all I can do is start hoping again. Oh, I had such confidence yesterday. That princess of Wales has cost me dearly, perhaps cost me my future. I will wait and see.

Well, the aftermath of my little experience last night hasn't turned out to be quite as devastating as I first thought it would. I had quite a horrendous time in the morning, but during the afternoon I took a trip to the city, and the visiting of the various bookstores of the city helped once again to refocus my mind on the important things. It has been my love of books which has kept me going at times during this whole escapade. Their sleek and finished appearance has indeed been an inspiration. I don't know what I'd do if I happened to lose the joy associated with books. They have really been a delight in at times a fairly bleak existence. I'm looking forward to a career as scholar. It sounds a bit strange talking of a career when there are times when I can hardly think properly, but I'm beginning to become optimistic about my future prospects. Even though my ability to write comes and goes, at least it is still coming from time to time. For a while there I thought I had lost the ability for good. I will really have to learn the use of words. That should be my main objective for the moment. To really immerse myself in the wonder of words, and to become proficient in their use. I just hope my writing abilities can handle the strain which is my life. I have a continual fear that I will lose them. I'm just hoping that their here to stay. I think what would make my life complete would be to once again appreciate the beauty of things. I was in David Jones today, and was looking at some very fine furniture, which usually inspires me greatly, and there was little response. I could still tell what I liked, though it seemed more from memory than anything else. I'm starting to visualise what my study will look like, and what more generally my house will look like. I know exactly the type of furniture which I will buy. Very scholarly indeed - English oak bookshelves, tables and chairs. Antique chests and wall units. And lots of books. I'm thinking of starting a library. Just a small one, but a library none the less. I have quite a few books at the moment, but I think to fill the four walls of a room would be my fancy. Well perhaps not the four walls, because I think I'll situate my library in the study so I'll have to leave room for the writing desk and the gentleman's chair.

It's truly amazing how fragile the mind can be. I've gained a very deep insight into this fact. There's not a day which passes in which my mind doesn't collapses in some way. There are such a variety of causes that its very hard to keep track of just what to look out for. This morning I woke up feeling very "alive", my perceptions had once again returned to me and I was starting to feel that my life once again had some sort of foundation. I then got up and walked around, and I must have walked just a little to fast and my mind just collapsed, or broke I think is the more appropriate word to use. The last year of my life has seen broken mind after broken mind, for no apparent reason. I think somehow my mind has opened up to the external world, exposing it to the vicissitudes of the physical body. Who would have though the mind could be subject to such physical constraints. It's a situation that is very difficult to describe to anyone who hasn't experienced it. I wonder if anyone else has experienced what I'm experiencing. There must be other people who have experienced similar things. I don't suppose there's anything like a support network, I guess it must be quite a rare situation. I live everyday with the fear of breaking yet another new mind.

Well, I've lost a part of my mind again. This time it seems to have been the part of my mind which can appreciate fine furniture. I was talking to someone, and I just happened to

Diary of a Schizophrenic

glance at a writing desk as I was talking to them. At the time the person was talking quite forcibly to me about some particular topic. And my mind just collapsed. I now look at the desk and there isn't that same sense of satisfaction one gets from observing a thing of beauty. It seems I am destined to lose every facet of my mind which gives me pleasure. I am hopeful that the sensation of pleasure at looking at such fine furniture will return in time. It has to, for it is one of the few pleasures which my poor mind is able to afford me. I am confident that it will return. I am wondering what new horrors are in stall for me in the near future. It seems as if whenever I get some of my mind back, that another part is whisked away. All I want to do is become a scholar and once again enjoy the finer things in life. Music, art, reading, writing. These are the things I live for, and I only hope I will not successively lose every faculty of appreciation regarding these pleasures. I find it very hard to describe the process as it happens to me, but I am trying my best. There is little left to me in the way of appreciation, but I seem to regain some of them at intervals. I've recently regained some enjoyment in the act of reading. The one joy left opened to me, although there were times when I'd thought I'd lost that to. I was just walking past some very heavy construction, and there was a workman using some drilling device to excavate a whole in the ground. It was quite a loud noisy devise and it seemed to affect my mind as I walked past. That's another way my mind is impinged upon, through sound. Harsh grating sounds seem to directly affect my mind. There are times when I think I may never recover from such attacks. But invariably my mind does recover. I am quite thankful that it does, for my mind will become my livelihood in the future, and I don't wish to lose it. There are times however when I fear the worst.

I just simply can't believe what's happening to me. All I did was take a sharp turn when I was walking and a part of my very being disassociated itself from my body, leaving me feeling quite empty of feelings. This phenomena just continues to throw unbelievably insidious tortures at me. This time it has robbed me of all my desires and aspirations. It's a very difficult thing to formulate into words, but that part of my being which left my body must have contained within it that part of myself which is concerned with desire. It has left a terrible void just below the surface of my consciousness. It has crippled my feeling capacities. I was just starting to return to some semblance of normalcy as far as perceptions were concerned, but now I fear I have taken a step into an unredeemable void. I have felt similar sentiments before, but this time I fear the worst. I don't know if I could ever get used to living like this. Once one has had the privilege of leading the higher life, one is hard pressed to live a life of any lower calibre. I guess I've been leading such a lesser life for so long now that such a prospect fails to impress upon me, but it just isn't the case. I yearn for the higher life, of study and contemplation - writing and reading. This is what I live for, and I can hardly endure such a meagre existence. But I must, for there is still the chance that I may emerge from this horrid condition to take my place within society. I have the gift of writing, which I believe to be still with me, so I must continue on to somehow seek out some form of existence. There seems little point in hiding away in any other way. All I can do is hope, and at least some of my hopes have recently been realised, no matter how briefly. There is still the chance that I may recover. But every time I do there is something, invariably, which draws back down to this dungeon of an existence. I was born to fly I believe, and to lead this life is something which grates against every fibre of my being, or ever fibre that is left I should rather say. What can be done is being done, so I should just sit back and try and enjoy myself. But how can one enjoy oneself when all avenues toward leisure have been blocked. I should stop fearing the worst and start living, but living for me means enjoying the higher life.

Well last night was yet another disaster in a long line of such disasters. It was the light fantastic last night which took me off guard. Although I must admit the whole day was quite an horrendous affair. One minute I would be enjoying the comforts of an adequately working mind, the next, due to some occurrence, I would be floundering on that uncharted reef which is sometimes my life. But I once again awoke this morning to find my mind was working quite well and recovered from the vicissitudes of the proceeding evening. I really should make an attempt to discover just how it is possible for light to play such a devastating role in ones mental well being. It seems quite a freak of nature that such an occurrence is at all possible. I can't even conjecture as to the nature of this phenomenon. It is an utter mystery to me, for surely the nerve ways are protected somehow form letting any damaging transmitter travel them. The mind surely cannot be that exposed to the elements. But unfortunately mine is. I would love to conduct some sort of study into the nature of such things but I am sure that literature on the subject would be quite sparse. I think I would rather leave it a mystery for the time being, and just try and live in its foreboding shadow. To make things infinitely more unbearable, my ability to write fluctuates with state of my mind. Although on the main I think it will remain with me, and not be lost as I have so often feared. That is one small consolation in a sometimes stark existence.

I was reading the letters of William Blake yesterday and it struck me how essentially human he was. Due to his poetry and prose I had always considered him to be something approaching a meta-human being. His lofty forays in the realms of eternity have always left me wondering how he might ever come down to take his place amongst the mere mortals who inhabit this earth. But reading some of his letters it is clear that his concerns and ambitions were clearly human. Although his mind would oft tally in those uncharted regions of abstract thought, there were distinctive times when he worried more about mundane affairs. His art was no doubt the over riding concern of his life, but I never guessed that he could be so human in nature. I guess gaining an insight into someone through their letters tends to de-mythologise them, bringing them down to the everyday. I still think nothing less of the great man, but it is good to know that he shared concerns that others of us do.

Paul Fearne

Just writing a quick note to see if I can still write. Oh what another horrendous day. It was trip to the art gallery this time that turned into a nightmare. This time it was the string phenomenon. I think I've already made an attempt at describing this horrible occurrence, but I shall endeavour to do so again. Just as I was leaving the building to catch a ferry toward the city, my mind seems to leap outside of my body and attach itself to the insides of the house. As I walk up the stairs and toward the ferry terminal, my mind is stretched along the length of the "elastic band" which has been created. I then get on the ferry and travel to the city, all the way being caught up in this horrible effect - my mind is continually stretched out of my body, all the way to the art gallery in fact. Such an occurrence leaves one feeling extremely "hollow" and leaves the mental capacities severely diminished. I'm actually finding now that I cannot type as fast, for the lack of thinking ability. My appreciation of the art at the gallery was once again impaired, but at least not quite as much as last time I was at a gallery. I find it very hard to describe exactly how the day's events have left me, but none the less it is still quite an horrific experience. My whole experiential capacity is affected, my thinking has actually become "smaller". This is the only way in which to describe the situation, that thinking has in someway become smaller. Thoughts no longer have the power to move me, in quite the same way that words are ceasing to move me. It is some sort of experiential deficit, lacking any foundations in the emotions. I think I would call myself an experiential cripple, as well as an emotional cripple. My mind has indeed taken quite a battering over the last few days, which is shame, because the last few days have seen some of the greatest improvements in my thinking capacity. I only hope that once again my mind can improve to at least give me some pleasure in life. I guess I crave some sort of stability, but not at the cost of improvement. I can withstand much mental tumult as long as there is the chance for improvement, for new and improved modes of thinking and awareness to emerge from the debris which is my life.

Diary of a Schizophrenic

My thoughts have once again led me to the type writer. I am just about to start reading William Blake's life story, something which I should have done a long time ago. I think gaining some sort of insight into the man's life will lend my own life some greater level of cohesion. There is little doubt I find the man fascinating, well his work at any rate.

Well last night could have proved once again to be a disastrous affair. I started to feel the perceptions again that I had six months ago, but I just knew that it was not to last. It was quite an exhilarating experience, once again having my mind back to some sort of serviceable frame. But again, as has happened so often, fate has struck me down, though I feel better this morning than I have for quite some time. All I did was to scratch my face, at was seems to be a very inopportune moment, and half my mind went dead. I guess it feels something like if someone has a stroke. It hasn't seemed to have affected any of my capacity, it just feels quite odd. And I have the feeling that it will affect my thinking capacities in the long term. Oh cruelty, tempting me with moment of pure mental joy, and then tragically taking them away. It seems to have the story of my life to date. Brief interludes with a strong mind, only to be denied any sense of mental stability. It just seems to be my lot in life to suffer these misfortunes. I feel as close now to being whole as I ever have, but at the same time it is so far away. I can only pray that the damage done is not permanent, and that I will once again recover to lead the sort of life I was meant to lead. I have a strong feeling that one day I will finally be free of these mental tortures, and I will sing to the world a great song of joy and release. The damage to my mind seems to have affected the poetic side of my mind, the creative side. What a strange sensation to lose half of your mind. I can almost live in the two different halves at different times, which is a strange thing to say. The damaged half is not very pleasant, although the strong half is quite open and free, giving me the sensation as if I was living six months ago. I cannot express the extent of my frustration at being so close to being free, and yet trapped once again in the mental tumult which I have as late become so accustomed. But this time it is quite different - strangely permanent. The other inflictions upon my mind have had a temporary quality, which has relived my troubled mind form thoughts of an eternity in this hell. But now I may be faced with a permanent affliction to my mind. Only time will tell, but I can only hope that it somehow wears away and is forgotten, because otherwise I feel as good as I have in a long time. Hope is all I have, and it seems as if this time it will not be enough.

Yet another disastrous day. The very fibres of my being are being torn asunder. There seems nothing sacred to this horrid affliction. I can but write my simple notes, and be content. I sit back and watch as I am tossed about upon the hard seas of fate. I am still unable to understand what is happening, or indeed how it is happening. The sheer force of the disruptive energy has disabled my life, which now resembles something of leaky life raft. The very arrows of time are pitted against me, and they are unrelenting in there pursuit of their prey. I am forced to take a backseat to these troubling occurrences, and find solace in something other than my life. These are indeed strange words, but drastic action is sometimes required. I would challenge anyone to lead my life for one single day - a challenge none would dare undertake, if they value their mind. I sometimes wonder what the causes of my sorrows may possibly be, but I am at a loss. My affliction is indeed a mysterious creation, if creation it can be called! I would rather call it a pitiful anomaly, a queer phenomenon. But these are but words groping in the dark, searching for some speck of sanity with which to paint a picture. There can be nothing in truth which may be said of such things, but that they are disabling. I can only ponder as to the value of a normal human life, for such things are but distant memories, echoing on a distant shore. What can I do that is not already done? My mother would have me seek help, but I believe none could help me. I have

Diary of a Schizophrenic

tried in vein to seek the write help, and all my tryings having come to naught.

I've just realised something about my writing. My mind has become stuck in some sort of rhythmic groove. All my sentences are structured alone the same rhythmic variations. Although as I write these observations I find myself extending that variation. I was quite concerned for a while there. I guess I am becoming paranoid about losing my ability to write after all the loss that has gone on in my mind. I know one is supposed to be short and precise when writing, but my love is to compose long winding sentences which explore in depth certain topics. With my ability to write still intact I feel I can go on living with some level of happiness. I just couldn't bear losing this ability it is the one gift which I've been given. To sample the joy of words is to enter a kingdom one does not soon forget.

I am so close to having my life back again. I can feel my mind struggling to regain its former potency. My reactions to certain stimuli are however continuing to fluctuate quite extravagantly. I can sometimes look at nice piece of furniture and gain quite a strong appreciation of its beauty, but at other times that ability is impeded. I can listen to the radio at times and "feel" the music as it travels through its scale of sensation. While at other times the music is quite dead and it fails to move me in the slightest. My mind is gasping for its former strength, but I find it continually slipping back into that dreaded realm of non-awareness. My surroundings have become increasingly important to me, while my appreciation of such environs is a bit fluctuating, at worst non-existent. I can feel my mind slipping into that rhythmic pattern again, and everything that I write is coming out the same. My sentence's structures have reverted back to this frustrating cadence. I know I can write in a less rhythmically constrained manner. I just hope that such a situation does not last indefinitely. For my writing is my life. I live to write.

The most amazing of things has just happened to me. I've just been reintroduced into the world of experience. I was on my way to have lunch with my mother when I began to notice a certain change in my perceptual interchange with the world. The trees seemed alive again, the houses had a certain "feel" and the people were again objects of my casual criticisms. I find it hard to relate just exactly what the change has been, for what I am left with is what people experience everyday. Although once again my mind was disturbed by some external force. A man was sweeping some dirt as I walked by him, and the noise severely impeded my thinking and conceptual capacities. It was a nightmarish occurrence, to have mind continually at the mercy of the external world. But I live in hope that this occurrence will only be a temporary one. I feel more the old self, the self that travelled to America and to Europe. Although this is a self which was much younger and less mature than the self I know today, I can still get used to the change. As long as I am allowed my perceptual capacities back again. I can accommodate any intrusion into the state of my mind as long as I can once again enjoy he external world. To see the world once again is something I hope never to lose. It sounds strange talking of losing the external world, but it has happened to me so often that I'm almost used to it.

I am at something of a loss to describe what I'm going through at the moment. I seemed to have regained my experiential capacities, but at the loss of some of my other qualities. It's very hard to describe just what has taken place. It feels like I've been placed in a sort of time warp, in which I've been transported back to a time before all of this began to happen. It seems to have affected my love of books in some odd way. I went into a bookstore yesterday and there just wasn't the same "pull" toward certain books that I had experienced before. But as some sort of trade off, I can now look at the window and appreciate the sunlight as it slants down from the sky, something I have been quite unable to achieve in the past few months. I'm still unsure of how to take such a change in my demure. I seem to have also lost the desire to write and research, things were quite fundamental to my make up. These underlying psychological forces in my have just seemed to vanish in a puff of smoke. I don't know whether to be quite disappointed about the passing of these things, or to be quite overjoyed at the return of some of my experiential capacities. It seems as if I can never get it just right. There's always something which holds me back from the sort of life that I wish to lead. The flow of words is not coming as fluently as it once had, and I find myself struggling to write these few words. My flair in writing also seems to be affected, I don't feel the same compulsion to use descriptive language as I once did. I guess I crave some sort of stability in this very topsy-turvey existence, but I am loathe to achieve it at the expense of those things which are most important to me i.e. my writing and reading capacities. I have begun reading Ludwig Wittgenstein's biography, and in strange way it has failed to move me greatly in the way in which it normally would. The descriptions of his early life would have been sufficient to make me quite interested, but it strangely left me a little unaffected. This man, who had such a dramatic influence over my philosophical interests, should in no way fail to move now.

I believe that I was possessed of quite something special. My philosophical capacities were very pronounced and my insight into some of the great minds was indeed in depth. I can only now pine for those long ago days when I was riding on the wave of philosophical insight, but it's a memory which I enjoy to have constantly occur in my mind. I guess I will never again feel that overpowering drive toward the philosophical. It's quite a shame that I won't get to write anymore from the depths of such insight. Ah, I miss those days.

Oh, why could my life not have turned out differently? I had so much to offer the world, and now I am nothing more than a senseless aberration. These are strong words, but they seem the only words which can express my current predicament. When one has experienced aspects of a higher and greater life, it becomes intolerable to live such a meaningless existence. One does not soon forget those flights into the wonderful space which is thought. There is no going back, life cannot hold meaning without those heightened appreciations. A normal life just does not suit my temperament, or what is left of my temperament. I was possessed of such strong passion and commitment to my ideals and I am now unable to even generate ideals. I just live life is in state of personality shock - having lost all those aspects of my personality which were so important to me, I simply live in a feelingless void. I went to a play last night, *Diving for Pearls* it was called. I could sense that it was a very good play. But I could just not become involved. All those things which makes one human were missing. All those little responses to emotional stimuli that are at the core of any viewing of a play. They were all gone. So that all that was left was a half felt idea that in some way the play was good. The acting, the dialogue, the drama were all there, but just not felt - not appreciated. Although at least I'm starting to realise what is missing. Small consolation at best, for the loss of so much of what constitutes me.

Today was quite an extra-ordinary day. I was finally able to appreciate the hues of a golden red sky as the sun was setting. We took a wonderful stroll down to the harbour side which was nothing less than immaculate. The world had come alive for a brief moment once again. We walked past the Hyatt Hotel and I could once again feel myself appreciating the fine furniture of the place. But more importantly, oh, the wonderful sky. The sea came alive, as did the harbour. I found myself quite unable to believe what was happening. I almost went into some sort of experiential shock at the opening up of my sensory capacities. But of

Diary of a Schizophrenic

course it was not to last. I caught a glimpse of some quite intense light reflecting from the water and my idyllic afternoon was cut abruptly sharp. But no matter, I think just the memory of those wonderful few hours will keep me going for some months. I am hopeful now that one day I will make something of a full recovery. My mind will once again display its potential. I feel so relieved that I am still able to enjoy the pleasures of summer stroll. I only hope the trend continues. It would be something of a tragedy to once again be consigned to that horrid void which has been life the last year. I am confident however of a full recovery. Only this morning I was unsure if I could ever find myself "alive" again. It would be quite something if I also could recover my philosophical interest. There is hope of such a recovery also, for I found myself having a rare insight into the work of Wittgenstein this afternoon. Just sitting down on the ferry I made a realisation of what Wittgenstein meant when he said that the world was made up of facts and not things. He was making reference to the role language plays in the perceiving of reality, that our perceptions are conditioned by the language which we employ to come to terms with our reality. Even to make such an observation is indeed encouraging. What a joy it would be to make such a double recovery, a philosophical recovery as well as a perceptual recovery.

I look forward to once again engaging in philosophical speculation. I am just writing a few words to ensure that I still have the capacity to write. I guess that I'm quite paranoid that one day my gift will desert me never to return. Because my mind is so exposed to destruction from external stimuli, I fear that one day that part of my mind concerned with writing and scholarship will one day depart. I sincerely hope it to be a groundless one, one that will leave me through the course of time. Though for the moment I live in a state of constant perplexment. It seems that every time my mind recovers some sort of normalcy something happens which reduces my capacities once again. I know these fears are indeed silly in their subject matter, but I am none the less still quite afraid. I am noticing that my writing has taken a certain rhythmic shape that is very difficult to break free from. Short sentences followed by comma'ed sentences. It's quite frustrating to be constrained by such a structure.

Well I've decided its time to take some sort of positive action to relieve this condition I've developed. I'm only disappointed that I didn't think of such a thing sooner. This morning was the last straw. After last night's incredible recovery, I was sitting on the couch enjoying my thoughts of yesteryear when someone started sweeping in the front portion of the villa. Well needless to say it once again destroyed the mental process that was happening and I was left with a decimated mind again. But no more will I stand for such intrusions into my mental state. It has gotten too much, I have lost just too much. I'm finally going to confess my condition and see if there is nothing which can be done. I think taking such action will at least allow me study with some foundation of stability. I guess that's all I'm after. I feel almost exited at the prospect of finally being able to lead something of normal life - not having to be continually concerned about when next my mind will be impinged upon. I may even be able to once again continue to learn the use of words which would be an incredible joy.

I am once again forced to venture to my keyboard in the hope that I haven't lost my ability to write. This fear is my constant companion, following me through every step of my life. This time my thinking capacities have been curtailed simply by eating an apple. I can't seem to grasp the complexities of the Wittgensteinian mind quite as easily as I had done before. Somehow eating that apple has short-circuited my thinking capacities, something which I had always feared would happen. The notions of 'language game', 'forms of life', 'family resemblance' float around in my mind searching for a meaning to append to, but eventually finding none they meander of the minds stage to find rest in some other pasture. If this remains the case then I will cease to live, my mind and its philosophy is my life-blood. To cease to understand philosophy is to cease to live life. This may sound somewhat drastic, but I jest not about such things. I have so little left in life, all I have is my love of philosophy and the arts. They are my life-blood, my reason for living. I can't comprehend life without them. But I have the sinking feeling that indeed I know must live a life without such things. I will wait and see what happens to my mind, but in the mean time I will write a quick synopsis of what I think Wittgenstein means by the above mentioned notions.

Language games - Language is "played" in the same fashion as a game is played. Language is acquired in a similar vein. One learns the rules of language and then in speech employs those rules as guiding buoys to secure coherent meaning. Each sub-species of the language is itself a language game. When conversing about the weather one is engaged in a different language game then when one is conversing on the subtleties of applied mathematics.

Private language - One comes to language via a set of pre-disposed behavioural traits which engender language acquisition. Pain language is a natural extension of pain behaviour - one initially cries in pain and then is taught pain language. This is Wittgenstein's famous private language argument.

Forms of life - Every individual partakes of a form of life, as do communities and animals. A form of life is that which constitutes a beings inherent make-up and conditions the modes of expression which that being may employ. People from two different cultures may share the same humanity, but there form of life differs in the set of predispositions which they may employ in meaningful discourse. Wittgenstein says of lion that if it could talk we should not understand it, for it shares a different form of life. It is the form of life one is engaged in that determines accepted modes of language use.

Well I guess I've convinced myself that I haven't lost the art of writing, nor the ability to engage in philosophical speculation. So I rest contented for the time being, though I know it shan't be long before I once again come to this very type writer crying that I have lost my ability to write.

Need I even put into words the events which have befallen me during the last few hours? I have once again been set upon by those most tragic of mental occurrences. I live not day by day, but hour by hour, waiting for those horrible moments in time when my mind reverts to its dilapidated state which by now I know so well. I can do nothing but endure such hardships as they befall me. After once again feeling my mind return to some sort of stable equilibrium, it again come crashing down, this time through the agency of reading a book. It seems as if it is the simple things in life which must be my downfall. I come to a point in life where I am feeling perfectly content with the workings of my mind, when something arises out of the everyday landscape to strike me down so tragically and unfairly. I know not how my mind has been affected this time, but affected it remains. It seems to have affected my reading capacities this time, reducing them to something of an inconsequential power. My comprehension skills, which had improved so remarkable, are now once again at a low ebb. I can only hope they recover to there previous levels. For it is my reading which remains the one joy open to me, and I sincerely hope not to lose it. I must wait again and see how my mind recovers, for inevitably it always seems to do so.

I am once again forced to resume my death watch over the keyboard. I can only hope once again that I am still in touch with my ability to write. My consciousness has again been dealt another serious blow, one which I may never recover from. My ability to read does not seem to be affected in the way that I feared, but my appreciation of philosophy has taken a battering that is indeed intense. Reading Wittgenstein's biography I am left without the same feeling

Diary of a Schizophrenic

as I had before. Something happened to my mind while I was reading an autobiography of William Blake. I cannot describe the process, but my mind has been left decimated. I can actually feel a large portion of my mind missing, and it seems to be that portion concerned with matters of scholarship. I can only now pray that I haven't lost my scholarly abilities. But it just isn't the same! - writing these few words has become very labour some. The thoughts and ideas which had come so readily are now labouring to come into existence. I find I am here making very little sense, but it is all my poor mind can muster. I feel I have this afternoon lost something very important, and I only hope that I can recover it. My mind has not recovered itself form my loss of emotion, so I am fearful that this situation may prove itself permanent.

Have the store of thoughts and idea's finally dried up? Somehow my mind does not "feel" the same as it had only a few hours ago. There seems something missing from its general makeup, something which has left a terrible void. I always seem to recover from such flights into the realms of mindlessness, but this time I am fearful that my mind has been dealt a serious blow - so serious in fact that it shall never recover. I have some sense of what happened as I was reading that biography of William Blake. That part of my mind concerned with reading, writing, and the conveyance of general ideas was somehow exposed to the words on the page in front of me, and then somehow was destroyed through the act of reading. I am at a loss to really understand how such a thing could have happened, and I now live in something of a state of absolute dread. My imaginative faculties have also been somehow affected, and scene's that I could easily bring to mind with clarity now struggle to register within my consciousness.

My mind is so damned fragile that I can hardly bear it a second longer. After recovering from the confines of that abominable void into which I was cast yesterday, I have once again been plunged into the depths of mental torture.

On this occurrence I simply flicked through a few pages of the book I was reading and my mind once again "broke". It has again affected my reading abilities which is fundamentally INTOLLERABLE. I have to be able to read to enjoy the shreds which remain of my life. I guess my mind is simply too fragile to continue with any semblance of normalcy. I am still hopeful however of one day being able to resume my studies with little or no impediments. In my present state this sounds indeed like a very lofty and ambitious goal, but my mind seems to be able to recover quite well form such destructive interludes. I almost felt back to some semblance of my former self this morning, and I am hopeful that such feelings will become a regular feature of my life. It felt good to be once again reading with some semblance of insight. I still miss my old life terribly much. It is not enough for me to simply live, I must be engaged in some sort of constructive thinking, some worthwhile mode of thought must make itself known to my consciousness, or all is lost. I have been encouraged by some insight into the workings of language, which gives me great relief form my current predicament. It is insight into the realms of philosophy which I think makes me the most contented. With such fanciful flights into the realm of thought, life fails to maintain any meaning. Again this may sound somewhat drastic, but it is the truth. I have not had much worthwhile come form my mind for a period of such length that it makes me terrified to think of it. I am continually encouraged however that things will turn around one day, and I will be left with my old mind again. This sounds all so far fetched in the light of my current state, but I must not give up hope. Hope is all I have, hope of a better life, one free of all this mental torture. Oh how many mental tortures have been devised to bear down on me. They seem innumerable.

What a sweet day! I have once again recaptured my philosophical abilities. I know not how they have returned to me, but I am grateful none the less. I spent the entire afternoon walking through the Botanical gardens considering the subtler points of language, in a Wittgensteinian sense of course. It all became so clear to me, how language shapes

Diary of a Schizophrenic

our perceptions and therefore our reality. It became paramount that I continue my study of the use of words, for it is in their use that one can truly be free. I can even envision myself going on to honours in philosophy now, even writing a thesis - given that my mind can somehow withstand the rigours of everyday existence. But baring any unforeseen occurrences - and I've had my fare share of those, I can be confident now of returning to my studies in philosophy with great earnest. Oh, it's been so long now, and I can hardly remember the last time I had any thoughts regarding philosophy, I thought my mind had just lost touch with those inclinations. But not so. I can only hope that my mind can withstand the vicissitudes of a normal life. I would love now to go to the symphony and celebrate, but again I fear my mind might again "break" and I would be left were I was, in that horrible nameless void!

I have now decided to set myself a few goals. It is pointless to live my life with no ambitions or motivations, and although the circumstances of my life change on a daily basis, I feel the guiding light of a set of goals would be infinitely beneficial. I guess I've had these goals now for some time, but just have rarely considered the possibility of actually fulfilling them. My main goal in the short term is to complete my honours year. If yesterday is anything to go by then I should have relatively little trouble. As long as that part of my mind concerned with philosophy can service the rigours of everyday life then I should be held in good stead. My longer term goal is to complete my PHD. There are times when I would think this an impossible dream. I just haven't the same insight into philosophy that I once had. But I will keep it as a goal just to keep going. As a part of these two ambitions I will endeavour to set up a study in the house we end up living in. With any luck the room will have a fire place and a small window. I will furnish the room in the tried and true study way, with all my favourite artists prints on the walls, and a nice big rug in the centre of the room. I have been imagining such a study for some time now, and I am quite excited about the possibility of it coming into reality. It will be quite some time before I will get the chance to have a room all to myself which I can properly outfit, but I am eager never the less. So these are my two goals in life, to complete an honours year and to complete a PHD - both in philosophy of course. I guess reading the Wittgenstein biography has got me once again interested in questions of philosophy. So I hope my mind can remain serviceable so as I can once again explore the complexities of the philosophical pursuit. I will attempt to lead the life of an academic, visiting art galleries, seeing plays, going to symphony, taking walks through the botanical gardens, taking drives in the country, and most importantly of all visiting the Gibson library and engaging in intensive study. I will have to accept that there will be days when my mind won't really feel like doing such things, but I am hopeful that these time will be very few and far between.

2/7/98

I have once again re-entered the world of experience. Oh the sights, the COLOURS, the wonderful greens of the grass, the blues of the ocean. It is truly a joy once again to be alive. I had forgotten just what it was like to be a normal human being. But now I remember, and oh what a wondrous day. It hasn't all gone my way though of course. On the way home from the state library on the ferry, a certain sound pierced my mind, somewhat affecting it. The damage however was not too drastic and I am confident of a full recovery. I still can't believe that such a state will last more than a few hours, but at least I have something of a future now. I should really be talking of futures before I've had a few days of this, then I can be confident that it is here to stay. I've had other re-introductions into the world of sense, but they have all come undone tragically. I am hoping this time that my experiential capacities will stay with me. I am confident now of being able to study, but not only that, to live life with some gusty. I am not getting confident just yet, we'll have to wait and see what eventuates, but at least it's a step in the right direction.

Diary of a Schizophrenic

3/7/98

I am continuing to read the biography of Ludwig Wittgenstein. It gives me great comfort and shows me just what sort of life I could have led if I had not had such an affliction cast upon me. I have once again taken a backward step, and I know not how to come to terms with it. I was simply reading when I got up and left a good portion of my being behind. These are the only terms in which I can relate what is happening to me. They sound strange indeed. It has once again left me lifeless and without motivation. When this sort of thing occurs it happens so suddenly and rips away at the very fibres of one's being. What sort of cruel torture is it, to have the very essence of a persons being so cruelly taken away. This has happened to me before and I am confident that I will make a full recovery. It seems that not a day will go by in which I do not somehow lose a part of myself. It is enough to drive one to utter despair. I have risked planning a number of goals for myself, and would be very distraught if they could not come to some sort of conclusion. I must remain hopeful that I can once again recover. Every time a piece of my being is separated from me, it seems to somehow "grow" back, leaving me feeling replenished and alive once again. There are just so many things which I have to be wary of. I will one day list them so as to come to a fuller understanding of the effects which they have on me. This latest affliction is just one in a long of things which deeply affect me. But I should not be too concerned, and yet I can be nothing but concerned. My dreams of completing my honours year are continually put in jeopardy by the fluctuating fortunes of my mind and being. It is as if fate were taking me to a place that contains my most vivid nightmares, eager to devour me without the slightest hesitation. But I must be strong and continue to be hopeful. I have experienced worse than this, and I will experience worse in the future, but I now that I will one day achieve my goals. Despite all that is happening to me I am confident that I can succeed.

What a wonderful afternoon at the gallery. I have regained my ability to appreciate fine art, and such a re-acquisition has indeed given life back to these weary bones. I could once again see the deeps hues of colour in all their amazing intensity. The works of art would leap out of their frames and beckon me to come and inspect them closer. It was an exhibition of British art, and I don't think I've seen since the Rembrandt exhibition such fine use of colour. I guess it was due to my re-found appreciative capacities that I was so taken by the colour of the exhibition. But of course my joy was to be short lived. I decided to have a coffee in the gallery cafe, which was something of a mistake. The warm liquid "broke" my mind again, and as quickly as it had come it was gone. It was quite an interesting sensation, for I could see a knoll of grass and was appreciating its colour, then I had my coffee and the grass no longer had the power to move me as it had. It was quite a shock, but one that I am now all too familiar with. I guess I am once again consigned to this abominable void which I have been inhabiting. But now there is hope, hope that I will once again live my former life - that is to say lead the life that I was going to live before all this happened. I simply cannot contain my excitement. I wish I could adequately convey the sense of wonder which I felt as I walked through the gallery surveying the hanging works of art. I guess it simply goes beyond words. Now that's something I haven't experienced for quite some time, the ineffable.

4/7/98

I'm somewhat looking forward to coming few months. I can at least now see some sort of future spanning ahead of me. My studies have given me a direction and a purpose which I have been missing over the past year. I'm so looking forward to beginning to write a thesis. It is something that I should have been doing some time ago. It took me quite an extended period to complete my B A, but now that it's over I can concentrate on writing this up coming thesis. I'm still concerned as to whether my mind is flexible enough to once again grasp the subtleties of philosophy, but I'm sure it will all come back to me once I begin my reading. I'm still having difficulty understanding higher order philosophical difficulties, but there are times when clarity pierces the darkness and I am able to once travel those old and trodden byways of thought. I guess reading the Wittgenstein biography has once again refocused me toward the more philosophical aspects of my study. I find his life truly fascinating and am eager to continue my readings of his life and work. I can see now what I saw in him all that time ago. His personality in some respects was reminiscent of mine before I was set upon by these troubles, but I guess the parallels are limited. He lead a life that perhaps I could have lead, perhaps not quite the lofty heights which he did, but similar none the less. His period of school teaching in the Austrian country side is something I could have envisioned myself doing at some stage in my life. But these are all just speculations, for I am left with this life and I am determined to make something of it. With a little luck I can still complete my honours year and then I will go from there. Reading the details of Wittgenstein's academic life have inspired me to once again contemplate a similar life for myself. I hesitate to speculate as to my future, with the fluctuating situation which I find myself, but one needs to establish goals by which one may live life.

5/7/98

What an incredibly extraordinary night I had last night. I was somehow granted a full re-introduction into the world of perception and experience. It seems strange to talk of having something returned which never should be lost. One would imagine that to simply live is to engage in the world of experience. But somehow my mind continues to be clouded so that external stimuli fail to register upon my consciousness. Well of course that is not entirely true, with the impact light and sound have upon me, but what I mean to say is that something such as tree fails to register the normal emotional and experiential response. There is just a deadness to these perceptual acts. The mind truly conditions our reality - something I have learnt with the utmost diligence. My continual fluctuations in and out of the sensory realm has indeed taught me the power of the mind in shaping reality. To have all those experiential capacities which a normal person would enjoy one day, and have them gone the next is quite a stark reminder of the power of the mind. Last night I felt some semblance of normalcy again, actually feeling as though I had required my "humanness". I remember looking at the people as I walked past them and once again feeling as though I belonged in the human race. It was a feeling of being on an even keel with those around me. I actually felt my sexual impulses return, another facet of my life which has been strangely dormant over the past year. I was once again conducting myself upon a human footing. But as is usual, the moment was to be snatched away all to suddenly. The dinner time conversion which we were engaged in was much too strong for my fragile mind to bear, and while the conversation continued I could feel my mind reverting back to its unperceptive state. To compound matters, as I was walking back from the restaurant to catch a ferry, I walked past a busker and my mind once again "broke". I have almost come to accept such occurrences as a usual part of my daily existence, though I am still hopeful that I can one day participate in everyday life without the constant intrusions into my mental state.

5/7/98

Well I am once again in Melbourne, having enjoyed my two weeks in Sydney residing with my mother. It gave me a chance to realise that there is the hope of a recovery from this seemingly hopeless situation. Also being with my mother let me blossom into something of what I would like to be. The wonderful hours reading biographies, listening to the radio, visiting art galleries and the like really invigorated me immensely. It was quite an eventful period, in which my mind revealed itself to be not yet lost beyond hope. There were times when I had felt as alive as any other in the preceding six months. Meeting some of my mother's friends made me realise just how I miss having someone who is interested in the same sort of things as I am. One lady had quite an extended knowledge of Wittgenstein and Bertrand

Diary of a Schizophrenic

Russell, so our conversation was quite riveting. She made me reflect once again upon the sort of life which I could have been leading, for she was quite an accomplished and well read lady. It is meeting people like that which really liven up one's existence. I guess I've always been quite a solitary figure, but essentially people need people. Having said this I could quite envisage myself living something of a hermit's existence, with just my cat and my books to keep me company. I seem to have no real need for anything of a close companionship. I guess the nature of my life does not allow it anyway. The continual mental torture which I endure on a daily basis is not something someone would wish to contend with in a friend for any extended period. I seem to be quite happy occupying myself with reading and trips to the botanical gardens - and of course my memories. It is my memories which keep me company, memories of a life that I could have lead. This sounds quite sad and tragic, but I guess I have more than just my memories. There are times when my mind reveals itself to be on the verge of full recovery, and then I thank myself that I am still alive.

6/7/98

What another absolutely extraordinary morning. My mind returned to its original state, entirely. I could hardly believe what was happening to me. I lay in bed just thinking about Wittgenstein and Bertrand Russell, and enjoying my new found perceptual capacities. The day was alive with all the mental happenings that should accompany the normal functioning of a consciousness. Oh what I've been missing. But my joy was once again to be short lived. I made the terrible mistake of going outside to enjoy the weather, when a shaft of sunlight pierced my mind. It left me once again with a "broken" mind. All the wonderful perceptions which had occupied my morning were rudely and not so subtly destroyed. So I am once again left in that horribly vacuous void which is my mind without perceptions. I find I am struggling against the language in my efforts to describe just what it feels like to fluctuate so wildly from one mental state to the next. It's like having your entire world thrown into confusion and darkness, then to have the darkness lift, only to have it once again descend. But I am now very confident that one day it will all be righted, and I will be able to enjoy my life in the fashion in which I should have. I feel so excited at even the prospect of once again returning to a normal life, though my life will never really be normal. I have too many plans and ambitions that can only eventual once my mind had returned to its proper state. Still it's frustrating having to live once again in this void, no matter for how long. But never the less I am encouraged. I just wish I could function in a normal way without having to be concerned whether my mind is going to break or not. It leaves me in quite a paranoid state, forever wondering when the next time I will lose some of the capacities of my mind. I am just thankful that such flights into the realms of non-perceptions leaves my everyday capacities intact. It's just the higher faculties which seem to be affected.

7/7/98

Well I'm afraid that part of my mind concerned with philosophy has taken something of a battering over the past twenty-four hours. It seems as if that shaft of sunlight that pierced my mind yesterday caused a lot more damage than I had first suspected. It left half my mind in a decimated state. It feels as if there is simply nothing left on the left hand side of my mind except scare tissue. Again words fail me, although scare tissue is quite an apt way of describing the sensation. Reading the Wittgenstein biography has once again become a stale affair. It is so frustrating to once again find a love in something and then have it taken away. I have something of a feeling that yesterday was a very important day in which I had the opportunity to once again live the sort of life which I believe I have been born for. But I guess it was not be. I only hope that I will receive another chance. My mind seems to functioning quite well today, but it doesn't have the same intensity of perception that it did yesterday. It was extremely silly of me to venture out into the sunlight with such a fragile mind yesterday. I am well aware of the effects which such sunlight has upon me, especially when my mind is recovering. I only hope that I can once again recover to

Diary of a Schizophrenic

that level again. It was quite a joy to be once again living a whole existence, no matter how briefly. Now I am once again forced into this subsistence existence. But by now I am quite used to it so I should be quite able to manage this time around.

9/7/98

Well my life continues on its roller coaster of a ride. The last few days have seen some very remarkable improvements in my mental outlook. But every time there is some headway made, something eventuates which causes yet another slide into that horrible abyss. My mind is simply too prone to external influences. The slightest sound can cause my mind to spiral into that void which is the realm of non-experience - where all my visual and sensual capacities are severely impeded. I can spend hours simply doing nothing so as to safe-guard my mind, and then the smallest thing can ruin all the headway that I've made. I think I have to set myself a certain standard of activity, and stick by it so as to ensure that I am continually occupied. If I am left to take these safe-guarding measures I will spend most of my waking life concerned with protecting my unstable mind. I am truly grateful for the times which are conducive to my mind feeling whole, but protecting these times has become so very tiresome. I will continue to look forward to time when my mind can "recover", but I must not stop leading my life. Things that can horribly affect my mind just have to be endured. The television is quite a good example. I can recover the entire day, and then simply sit down to watch some television and I can once again be left where I was at the beginning of the day. But the catch being that if I don't at least do something to relax, like watching some TV, then I spend all day sitting around in my room, which has become quite tiresome. I must get out and somehow enjoy life. This inevitably means living on the edge continually, living on the edge of experience, forever fearing that something will happen to affect me. But I must not be concerned. I must continue to lead my life is some sort of constructive fashion. Even reading a book can "break" my mind, it really doesn't take very much. Listening to music can also be very damaging to my mind, depending on the state in which it's in. That's the thing, all these occurrences are very temperamental, and I can never be sure when something is going to affect me. But I must live on regardless.

10/7/98

Its quite amazing, but I seem to have re-acquired my emotions. It feels quite strange to once again be involved in the emotional world after such a long absence. I could hardly believe my feelings as it were. I look forward now to enjoying all the normal human emotions that people feel, that I haven't felt for too long a period. Fear, joy, excitement - things I haven't felt for almost a year. The re-acquisition of my emotion base has enhanced my memory faculties, allowing me to once again remember just what my life was like before this terrible affliction made itself known in my life. I was quite an emotional young man. I could feel things quite intensely and overpoweringly at times. I don't think I'll ever be able to once again feel emotions on quite that level again, but I'm glad to have them back never the less. I still have an incessant paranoia that I will once again lose my emotions, but I am sincerely hoping that such fears are entirely ungrounded. Even though my mind continues to be an incredibly unstable thing, I'm sure there is enough there to keep my emotions intact. I guess I am so "excited". It feels wonderful to be able to write that I'm feeling excited, something which I haven't felt for too long. I guess this means I can once again look forward to certain events, another thing which has been absent for just too long.

13/7/98

It's been an incredibly long and strenuous few days. In fact the entire week has been fraught with difficulties. Over this period I have seen the fortunes of my mind vary wildly. I don't even live form day to day anymore, but form hour to hour. My mind has become so extremely sensitive to the

Diary of a Schizophrenic

external world that I can hardly even recall a period of more than two hours where my mind was not affected in some way by some external source. I have however felt some very strong moments of recovery amongst this tumult. There was a brief period, and I accentuate the term "brief", when I almost felt my mind back to the same levels as before all this started to happen. It was quite amazing, it was as if I had been placed in some sort of time warp and I was back to where I had been six months ago. It feels quire odd talking in such a fashion, but I am at loss to talk in any other terms. How can I describe the pits of experiential inertial which I have frequented of late, and how such journeys have left the state of my mind? I find myself struggling against the language trying to adequately describe just what is happening to my mind. I have not given up hope of some sort of recovery however, although I think I will need to employ some sort of assistance. There must be other souls who have experienced just what I have experienced, and hopefully there will be a body of knowledge to which I can refer. I am at a loss to know just what measures can be taken to rectify the situation, but I am certain there is something which can be done. I can be silent no longer, and I must face any reducible which may eventuate from my honest search for some sort of cure. I am sure that there will be few who could believe such a fanciful story of extended hypersensitivity. But I must be strong.

15/7/98

Well today I am feeling perhaps the most refreshed that I have for quite some time. My mind, although having taken a battering this morning when I ate a piece of toast (of all things), is feeling quite stable. I can slowly but surely feel my experiential capacities returning. Just to be able to sit and enjoy the sunlight as it drifts through the kitchen window is a joy that I haven't experienced for far too long. I get terribly paranoid though when my mind does recover, for I know that it is only a matter of time before it once again reverts back to that void state, in which there is no experience whatsoever. But for the time being I can content myself with having my mind back to something of its original stature. I'd forgotten what it was like to experience things in a fresh and vibrant way. It is truly the simple and free things in life which are the most enjoyable. I sincerely hope that I don't once again slip back into that horrible world were there is no beauty and no pleasure. That is a world in which I have lived for too long now, and I can't bear the thought of having to go back there to live. I'm even starting to think in terms of the future, allowing myself that luxury. I can see the future stretching away before me, and it will either be a very joyous one, or a very tragic one. For the time being I feel that it is heading at least in the right direction. There can't be too much more go wrong than has gone wrong over the past, so I guess I am prepared for all eventualities. I guess I am prepared to live in that void if that is the only option I am given, but I can see other possibilities now that don't involve those eventualities. I can see myself now studying for quite some time and really getting a lot out of it. That seems to be the only thing which I have my sights set on, is to study, and I guess the re-acquisition of all my experiential capacities. Both now seem like possibilities, and if they do eventuate I could not be happier. But I shouldn't really be thanking my lucky stars just yet, for I don't seem to be out of the woods just yet. There is still a long way to go before I can say that I have recovered, and I don't even like bandying that term 'recovered' around.

16/7/98

Well another day dawns upon me and my mind seems to be holding up to the challenge. My life has ground to a halt though as my paranoia about breaking good minds reaches a crescendo. I am loath to do anything that will expose my mind to the world, and so I at times do absolutely nothing but stand around and think. I think mainly about my studies and what I'm going to do with them. Such thoughts keep me occupied for quite some hours. But I must be determined not to let my life continue this way. I have to start living again, even though this might mean losing some of the tremendous progress I've made over the past few weeks. I

Diary of a Schizophrenic

just can't stop living, though that is the very thing which I've done over the past week. I've become to overprotective of my mind. It's easy to say, however, that I will start to live life though when almost every step which I take in life is fraught with the danger of once again being brought back to the void. Every time I see my mind recovering I scurry back indoors and lock it away, thereby hoping to ensure that it doesn't go away again. But this is ridiculous. When my mind is recovering I should be taking the opportunity to live the moment, for I don't know when I shall get the chance again. For the times when my mind is at its best are sometimes very momentary, and I should be trying to live those moments for all they're worth. But once again its easy to write such things, but much harder to live them. Recently however my mind has been making some very substantial recoveries from seemingly hopeless situations so I live in hope that such trends continue. It's also very hard to gauge exactly what is going to affect my mind at any given time. Sometimes the television does, other times it doesn't. Sometimes drinking a drink does, or brushing my teeth does, and other times they do not. So I can never be really sure what's going to affect my mind and what isn't, so I am left in a continual state of concern. I think I have to adopt the attitude that there will be times when things are going to affect my mind and I just have to live through them and accept and hope that my mind can recover.

17/7/98

Last night I enjoyed the most incredible recovery. It seemed as if I had been transported back through time to a period when I was truly alive. It's difficult to describe just how my perceptions fluctuate from the normal to the sub-normal, but it's an experience which is quite disconcerting. I went to give William a lift to Moonee Ponds so he could return a video when my mind started functioning again in its old mode. But once again the joy was short lived as an innumerable number of lights and sounds impinged themselves upon my mind and dismantled all the good work that had been done. Such returns to the land of the living give me much hope and comfort that things, in the end, will right themselves. There are times now, in fact quite extended periods, where I can imagine myself living something of the life which I want to lead - that is studying to the very highest level. It seems almost incredible that I could even contemplate such things given what I've been through and am still going through, but I truly believe things are eventually turning around. I guess I am still living to a certain extent from one day, nay one hour to the next, but at least those hours are become more and more filled with thoughts that had been absent for too long. Thoughts of actually being able to lead the sort of life I want. I actually think quite a lot about study and how I am going to really enjoy this coming honours year. It still hasn't really dawned on me that I've finished my B A, it's been such a part of my life for so long. But the study continues so it isn't over yet. I'm even starting to contemplate living by myself for a period. I think though I would turn into something of a hermit if I was to live by myself. But is that necessarily a bad thing? I've always enjoyed my own solitude and having the total freedom of living by myself might indeed be what I need. I don't want to become too introverted though, despite the fact I am quite an introverted person as it is. Still the idea has become very appealing. I would be able to set up my house in exactly the way I like it, I can just imagine it. I know exactly the type of furniture I would like.

20/7/98

Well the desire to study philosophy has somehow left my heart. It's incredibly unfair and heartbreaking. Just as my life was starting to take some shape and direction, this loss of desire strikes me to the very core. Where once there were pangs of pleasure at studying the great philosophers, there is now cold stony blankness. It seems unendurable that I must live without that which has given me so much comfort over the past months of bleak non-experience. When my outer world came crashing down, I could always turn to the inner world of philosophy to comfort and console me. Just imagining myself in the Gibson library studying away gave me immense pleasure. But now where there was once pangs of pleasure, there are now pangs of trepidation. It seems unimaginable that it should turn around so fast, that I should be left with nothing of the joy which I once felt in my pursuits at philosophy. I live in hope that I will one day recapture that same motivated inspiration which had kept me company for such an extended period. But for the time being I am consigned to that inky blankness of non-philosophy. I have traded now my inner world for my outer, for I am now able to enjoy my surroundings once again. Beams of sunlight, while still troubling me endlessly, in the right condition now give me some pleasure. The thought of walking through a park, or even travelling, now gives me a sense of the wonderful as before it left me only coldness. But it seems as if my life can never conjure some sort of harmony.

21/7/98

Well last night I regained my philosophical interests, only to lose them again the very next morning. It's quite frustrating as I watch my life return to some semblance of what I would wish it to be and then watch it slide back into that no man's land. It happens on a continual basis, my mind is just too open to external influences to remain stable. It seems strange though that these external stimuli should affect my desires and aspirations. For one day I may be filled with octets of desire to study up to the highest level, and the next that desire has entirely left my heart. Such fluctuations seem to be conditioned by the state in which my mind is in. I guess I could put it down to a temperamental flux, but I believe it is truly more than this. The loss of desire is too marked, too acute, to be simply the result of emotional change. There is a fundamental change in my heart which occurs, a fundamental differentiation in my emotional base which has its cause in the mind. I am just thankful that these changes are nearly always rectified at some stage in the future. A loss of philosophical interest is nearly always accompanied by a rise in some of interesting facet of my life. On this occasion it was the visual arts which took its place.

But the visual arts have always only been an interest, and never the sole motivating force in my life. It is philosophy which truly gives me a sense of doing something worthwhile, and to lose its sweet comfort is a tribulation I can hardly bear for too long a period. It is absolutely awful to have to live an entire day without the joys of philosophy residing in my heart, and yet it has happened and I must only hope that it returns yet again. There simply is no replacement, nothing in my life which is an adequate substitute. The other parts of my life provide stimulating relief from the circumstances of my life, but it is philosophy which is truly my love. I sometime wonder, even when the desire has returned in full, whether my mind is still capable of the highest from of abstract thought. A single month ago I would definitely had said no, but I think there is still a measure of flexibility within my mind to allow it to engage in such speculation.

22/7/98

Well my beloved philosophy still seems to be taking a hiatus. It really is quite a frustrating situation. With my philosophy in tow I could quite possibly make a life out of this troubled existence. But I guess for the time being it just simply is not to be. I still live in hope that at some stage it will return to me in its full splendour - an overriding passion that takes no prisoners. I am currently making a full recovery from the troubles I have experienced in the past and it is a shame that philosophy can't come along for the ride. Well maybe there is still room in my heart for philosophy, I don't think it's quite a foregone conclusion yet. I still have my honours year to look forward to. And I will be writing my honours thesis on Wittgenstein so I better start feeling some passion at some stage or I think there is going to be trouble. I am having trouble visualising myself studying in the Gibson library, an act which in the past has given me much joy. It just doesn't seem the same. There aren't those pangs of anticipation that were prevalent in my past visualisations. Such imaginings have kept me going over quite a troubled period, and just when things are starting to look up I hope not to lose them. But I guess I'm used to losing those things which are dear to me, but I have been lucky in that they have always returned to me in full. I look forward to the day when my philosophy reigns supreme in my passions once again and leads to the promised land of academic excellence. This is my dream, and I can only hope it eventuates. So for the time being I live in a space which contains some joy, the joy of living with my external world again, but also with some trepidation, as that part of my inner world which was so important to me has departed.

23/7/98

Last night saw yet another set back on my road toward recovery. I had finally achieved a certain level of reading awareness as I read Wittgenstein's biography. I could feel myself becoming immersed in the man's life and his philosophy. But my new found reading capacities were to be short lived as the air vent which conducts the central heating was turned on. The sound "broke" that part of my mind which was concerning itself with the act of comprehension, and as a result I have found that my ability to understand higher level concepts and ideas has been impeded. Well not so much understand, I am still able to think on such topics, but just gaining the comprehension from the written word has become difficult. As if somehow it was that part of my mind concerned with reading that had become active and was foremost in my mind at the time when the sound impinged upon my consciousness. After the event I attempted to read quite a detailed and subtle argument concerning Gestalt psychology and I found myself unable to understand a word. I can actually feel where that part of my mind was before it was destroyed - it is quite a strange sensation. It was part of the right hand side of my mind if that makes any sense. At any rate I am hopeful that such effects are only temporary and that I may once resume my studies in philosophy. For it seems my desires in philosophy have returned, only to be thwarted now by a lack of ability. It seems this is destined to be the story of my life, brief interludes of mental awareness, punctuated by extended periods in which my mind functions in a sub-standard fashion - well at a non-heightened level at least. It all seems to me quite a frustrating and at times unendurable situation. But I must endure, for there is still the chance that I may one day indeed recover to the level that I dearly have hoped for - resuming my studies in their full intensity. I have the occasional glimpse of what my life could possibly become and it keeps me in strong hope for a bright future.

24/7/98

I'm finding that my desire to study and research has reached a point where it is only half hearted. I have half my philosophy back as it were. It's quite tantalizing to see half of that special gift which I had, to see it working its magic in this half state. Last night I thought indeed it returned in its full glory, but I woke this morning to find it teetering on the verge of being snuffed out once again. But I guess I am glad for the semi-return of my scholarly aspirations. For there's only one thing that I really wish to do, and that is to study. But I will find it increasingly difficult if I cannot muster the appropriate passion for the tasks at hand. What once instilled in me great pleasure, the study of Wittgenstein and other writings on the philosophy of language, now only half interests me. It is quite an intolerable situation. But I guess I can't be too greedy and expect my life to turn out perfectly. I have my perceptions back and can once again appreciate the beauty of the world around me, so that is a blessing I should truly be grateful for. I am not suffering any physical ailments, nor am I suffering from the pangs of unrequited love. Just the half loss of something special that I once enjoyed. I guess it can be endured so long as I have my outer world to keep me company. If I can't study with the same passion then perhaps I might travel and see if the desire returns after a lapse of time. For perhaps this loss of desire is simply the burning out of something which I have relied upon for too long a period. But I have still have the memory of what it was truly like to be dreaming of the great joys of intensive and unadulterated study, but that perhaps makes things all the more worse to now live in a world without such passion, or with half that passion. My life now just seems to be drifting along without the guided direction that it once enjoyed, for I always knew what I wanted to do, it

Diary of a Schizophrenic

was just a matter of not being sure whether I could do it. Now I can do it, the passion has departed my heart. But as I've said, I guess I must be thankful none the less. For I have lived a life that experiences no joy whatsoever, so to live a life of half joy is better to lead one of no joy at all.

26/7/98

I have had quite an eventful forty-eight hours. I have seen the return of my ability to philosophise with a vengeance. I have experienced some quite deep and profound insights into the nature of philosophy and language, some of which I am beginning to jot down in a journal. I had thought my mind no longer capable of such flights into to the realms of thought, but I was sorely mistaken. My life has once again achieved some sort of equilibrium, with my desire and my ability to do philosophy returning in abundance. I can hardly believe my luck. It is as if my life has emerged from the ashes and is resuming where it had left of. I am still incredibly open to my environment, so I am still extremely wary of being to confident of a full return to my former self, but for the time being there is nothing to do but enjoy my new found abilities. I am in continual fear of losing them again, but I must be strong and believe that everything will turn out for the best. I have struggled for so long now that I can hardly remember a time when I have enjoyed myself for any extended period. But I shall allow myself five minutes of enjoyment, enjoying the possibilities that are now open for me, possibilities that were, up until only recently, very closed to me. The prospects of continuing my studies in philosophy are very appealing now, and I look forward to the next six months of reading for my thesis. I shall read everything that I possibly can on Wittgenstein and the philosophy of language. I shall diverge occasionally and read some of the work of Davidson, Dummett, Grice and Tarski and maybe even a little Derrida and Chomksy. I will devote the next six months to an intensive study of language, and will see where that shall take me. I am hopeful that my understanding of language will be heightened to such an extent that I can do very well in my theses. I'm glad that I finally have a little bit of direction that I can follow. I think the philosophy of language is where I will most likely spend all of my academic time, so I should become as familiar with it as I possibly can.

27/7/98

I was quite surprised at the strength of my mind yesterday. To live with such a mind on a permanent basis, there's no telling what I may achieve in my studies. But as is usual it was not to last, although this morning I am once again feeling quite strong. I need not go in to the circumstances in which my mind lost its new found strength, suffice to say it was quite an uncomfortable experience. But I am once again feeling as if I can tackle all those difficult and subtle philosophical questions (which are not really puzzlements at all, but merely misunderstandings of language). At any rate, I feel once again able to tackle all the intricacies of the philosophy of language. Although I have no mind for logic, which is quite a large part of understanding this branch of philosophy, I can still see myself making some large advancements in my understandings. I began my study of Wittgenstein yesterday. It may well be too early to begin, for I have another six months to go before I begin writing my thesis, but my mind was so much on fire that I thought I'd better strike while the iron was hot. It proved quite fruitful to study Wittgenstein in such a state of mind, for his work seems much more lucid when one has a grasp of the ways he was thinking. Not that I really understand him yet, but I feel it is just a matter of time before I make a break through and really understand him - in the same way I understood him a year and a half ago. I think all those insights are still in my mind, their just laying dormant, waiting for me to resume my study. I am excited at the prospect of once again coming into to contact with such thoughts. I have been quite pleased to see my mind again working on problems of philosophy. It was been an absence which has lasted too long. All that I've been through almost seems worthwhile now that I can once again think about those sort of puzzlements. Now all I have to do is hope that it lasts, and that I am able to continue my investigations for some time into the future. For my honours year is still another six months away, so I hope that I can continue well past the end of my honours year, even on to do a PHD.

28/7/98

Well life progresses relatively smoothly. Again last night my mind allowed me to gain something of a glimpse of a larger world. I again had some very intense insights into the nature of the mind and language. I am hopeful that these insights continue so I can compile some sort of written work on them. I guess most of these insights have been made by greater men, but it is still exciting to be making them none the less. My mind is still very prone to assaults form the external world, but I seem to be managing them none the less. It makes it all worthwhile, having my desire to study back, my ability and my mind. My philosophy has been given a new lease on life. But I must be wary of becoming to over-confident, for it can all come crashing down very suddenly. But I must not be a pessimist and must remain confident that the worst of the days are behind me. I can look forward to a world in academia for the near future. My understanding of Wittgenstein grows day by day, but I must be careful not to get to carried away and burn myself out. The writing of my theses is still six months away, so I should supplement my studies of Wittgenstein with other things to allow me to remain focused for the entire six months.

29/7/98

I had a fantastic afternoon at the university today. My mind had finally achieved something of its full potential, and I strode through the grounds brim full of confidence. I spent some time in the university Book-room, surveying all the books on analytical philosophy which I am hoping to buy at some stage. I really felt as if I finally belonged, and that I had arrived at my life's calling. But once again I am hesitant to sound such optimistic strains, for I know how easily things can go wrong. But I should let such thoughts take away from my wonderful memories of this afternoon. I topped of the day by reading some commentaries on the work of Wittgenstein, and although I found it quite heavy going (my mind didn't seemed to be keyed into its understanding of Wittgenstein today), I still enjoyed the experience. This is how I wish my life to proceed. Afternoons at the university followed by periods of reading and then of writing. There are some moments when everything just falls into place, and this afternoon was one of those. My yearning to study the works of Wittgenstein has been diminished somehow though. It's as if wishing to study all the other analytical philosophers has somehow done an injustice to the mind and his love has exited my heart. But I am sure it is simply a temporary exodus, and that he will return in time. I dare say its uncomfortable to live a single day without my love for Wittgenstein's work, but I guess these things are temperamental, and the loss of desire being simply a fleeting occurrence. In the next few days I pick up a print of Wittgenstein I had framed, so that should inspire me to greater heights of Wittgenstein scholarship. Over the next six months, to prepare for my thesis I should write a few brief synopsis of my understanding of Wittgenstein, just to keep my writing brain in functional order. That may well be difficult to achieve, but I must try never the less. His work is notoriously difficult to understand, but I think I am coming to something of a higher understanding of the man and his work.

30/7/98

What did I write yesterday? A higher understanding of Wittgenstein! Well today that achieved understanding has entirely departed, and I labour over the works of Wittgenstein without a shred of such treasured comprehension. My how ones fortunes may change in such a short period. Yesterday I was ready to conquer the world with my valuable insights into philosophy, and now my mind has dried up again. There is no longer that pang of excitement at making those discoveries of Wittgenstein's thought. It seems that my having bought another book on

Diary of a Schizophrenic

the philosophy of language has somehow done an injustice to the man, and so accordingly he has left my heart. I sincerely hope this dreadful situation does not persist for any length of time. Well I guess I have six months to go before I write my thesis so there is plenty of time for a recuperation. But each day that goes buy without my heart set on discovering what Wittgenstein thought is hard to bear. This is perhaps a little melodramatic, and perhaps a little short sighted, but what can I do. My life yesterday was perhaps the most perfect it had been for quite some time, and I am loathe to leave such a warm embrace. But yesterday was another day, and I must come to terms with what has happened to day. I can only hope that circumstances present themselves in the same fashion again in the near future.

31/7/98

Well my studies are progressing very well. I have encountered Frege and am trying my best to come to terms with his thought. It is quite complex and quite brilliant, though not of the quality of genius as Wittgenstein's work is. Frege's distinction between the 'sense' and 'reference' of a word, combined with identifying the idea of a word and the thought of a sentence, were master strokes of their time. Though such insights have now been superseded it seems, they still provide a valuable account of the workings of language. I must be careful that I do not burn myself out on this stuff, though I find it immensely fascinating. I have to stop myself reading too many articles a day, so that I can at least absorb some of the complexity of the works I am reading. And I must remember also that my mind is still very fragile, so that to complex work may in fact be retrograde to my remarkable recovery. Though I can hardly help myself when it comes to the philosophy of language, but I must be careful none the less. I still have six months to go before I write this thesis, so I must time my run. But I am so interested now that it seems a shame to let that impetus go to waste. So in the short term I will study my philosophy of language and hopefully not burn myself out - and also not impede my recovery. I am planning to fully master the *Philosophical Investigations*, reading them a number of times until I have grasped what Wittgenstein is trying to say. This will be no easy task, for his work is notoriously difficult, but I seem to have some sort of ability in understanding (ah, but what is understanding?) Wittgenstein's thought. I cannot wait until I begin writing my thesis. I plan to have a full understanding of analytical philosophy and all those philosophers who have contributed to it, so that I may give a appropriately in depth appraisal of Wittgenstein's work in relation to the philosophy which preceded, surrounded, and came after it. So these are my intentions, which I hope will come to fruition over the course of the next few months.

2/8/98

I had the most remarkable few days in Canberra this weekend. I met up with a friend who I had not seen for some time and we had a wonderful time discussing the finer points of art and law enforcement. I am not a great admirer of Canberra, but I have to say the weather was quite splendid and the place was resplendent with greenery. We went to the National Gallery and took our time over the exhibitions. There is not enough renaissance art there for my liking, and far too much modern art. But what was there from the renaissance was quite amazing. A gorgeous ceiling painting by Tiepelo, and great portrait by Rubens were on display, and it was all I could do not to stop myself from ogling. Though these were the only paintings of any value there (my humble opinion anyway), it was still quite pleasant walking the grounds with my friend Edward and discussing the art that was surrounding us. I had never really had much of an appreciation of sculpture, but I saw the most wonderful sculpture of a little girl, I just wish I could remember the name of the sculptor. At any rate, after our little excursion through the Gallery, I headed of on my own to the National Library. Unfortunately the lending system was not functional on the day I was there, so I had to content myself with reading some of the reference material. I found a very comprehensive encyclopaedia of language and linguistics which listed and gave accounts of all the leading philosophers of language (except Derrida, which I guess is not surprising). So I spent the best part of three and a half hours reading through it. They also have a very extensive collection of Wittgenstein criticism, which was very encouraging. During the research for my thesis for next year, I may well travel back to Canberra and take advantage of the sheer range of works which are in storage. There were some very familiar names amongst the collection, but also a lot that I had never before set my eyes upon. So I am very encouraged at the range of material I have to select from. Though I must be careful and not read too much. For although the reading of materials is crucial for a successful thesis, I believe there is a thing as a glut of information. I have already read quite extensively, so I must just be careful not to step over that line and become glutted.

3/8/98

I have begun reading Goethe's *Faust*. It something I should have perhaps done a long time ago. It's a book I really would have enjoyed reading a year ago. Some of the themes and concerns which are presented are very close to a lot of the things I was concerned with at that stage in my life. But it is still none the less an interesting read now. Well the world has come alive for me. I am once again able to "feel" my surroundings. I know this sounds odd to say, but that capacity had been strangely dormant now for some time. I don't know just how to describe the reacquiring of this capacity, suffice it to say that it has improved my life immeasurable. I will have to wait and see if such an occurrence will endure, but I am hopeful that it will. My surroundings seem once again alive, and even asking a walk through the university grounds has taken on immeasurable delights. The sky and the trees seem once again imbued with something of a vitality which had been absent for the past six months. I am now able to once again appreciate poetry, and especially the detailed descriptions of the immediacy of the world.

4/8/98

The world continues to open its doors to my perceptual capacities. The grass seems ever so green, and the sky, the wonderful sky. I have never seen such hues presented in nature before. I only wish that I could once again experience the wonders of a sunset, but I fear that the piercing light would set me back to that void state which I dread so much. So I live without the pleasure of the sunset, but there are many more pleasures which I can enjoy now that I have my perceptual abilities back. The idea of travelling now appeals to me, though I am not sure if my mind would be strong enough to endure the hardships of the travelling life. While I was in Canberra I once again given to just simply watching the world around me as it past me by. Lake Burley Griffith was particularly alluring, with the various government buildings surrounding the lake side. It was quite a sight. I am hardly a great fan of Canberra, it simply doesn't have the charm and grace which the older cities exhibit. But the Lakeside was particularly beautiful. It has been quite some time since I've taken the time to simply sit and enjoy the world. As a result my appreciation of poetry has been greatly heightened. Wordsworth in particular, with his fanciful descriptions of the natural, has taken my interest. But I am very wary of his attitude toward books. "Lay your books down", indeed. I guess he was so overcome with the grandeur of the world that he has wont to put down his books for a direct experience. Which is a fair enough attitude, though one that I can't subscribe to. However, given my reintroduction into the world of the senses, I may well come to enjoy the world more than my books, though I can hardly see that happening. I feel there will be a wonderfully complimentary relationship between the two in which each will lend to the other so that my reading will enliven the world, and the world will give life to my reading. For I have lived in a lopsided place for too long, and it is time to once again even the scales. I have taken to reading in the mornings, followed buy an afternoon of worldly activities (university, bookstores, botanical gardens), then evenings of watching television, and then perhaps some more reading. It's a life that suits me well and is quite balanced. I do not become glutted with reading, nor do I become sick of the world. The television allows me the time I need to recover from my readings, as do my various expeditions out of the house. As a result of this regime I am finding that days are passing me by at an alarming rate, and that there is nothing I can do to stop it. Maybe however this is just a consequence of my gradually aging, for I have heard that once one ages to a certain level, then time itself seems to speed up beyond measure. Well perhaps I have now reached that stage, where my life will be consigned to something of a blur.

4/8/98

Well today was indeed a grand day. The sun was shinning, and the birds were a chirping. My mind, having recovered its full perceptual capacities, allowed me to glimpse the world in a way in which I have not done for some time. To make the afternoon that much more perfect I re-established my acquaintance with an old friend. We were perhaps in danger of drifting apart, but our lives have once again crossed paths and I can foresee a very meaningful friendship eventuating. She has taken to her studies with much gusto, and has achieved excellent results. I fully approve of her application and endeavour in achieving such high scholarly standards. Such accomplishments have inspired me to greater heights of scholarship, as I endeavour to research for my chosen field of study for my thesis next year. I really can't wait to begin, and have already purchased quite a few books on Wittgenstein. Today in fact I was quite happy to find a Wittgenstein dictionary, an invaluable aid to my studies. The explanations and descriptions are very detailed without being overly complex. The analysis of key terms is highly lucid and easy to comprehend.

5/8/98

Well it's quite an extraordinary day at the moment, and I can hardly wait to set forth and experience its splendour. The sun is once again shinning and there is a blue sky awaiting my perusal. I have finished my morning reading session and am looking forward to tackling the new day. I have just completed *Faust* and enjoyed it quite a lot. The lyrical play which imbues the work is surely a credit to Goethe's imaginative capacities. The story was difficult to follow at times as it jumped from one setting to the next. There didn't seem to be any coherent plot structure. No this is not true, for there was Faust's love for Margaretta which provided the main stay of the action. I was not expecting a love story when I began reading, though I was pleasantly surprised to find one. I guess I was really anticipating a solid pseudo-philosophical journey through all the larger questions of life, and although there were elements of such ventures through the story, they were not the main focus of the drama. It's been some time since I've read a piece of literature, in fact too long. I guess I've been quite content to immerse myself in philosophy, and let that passion takes its course. My understanding of Wittgenstein continues to grow, and I look forward with much anticipation to the coming months when I may in fact master his thought. Perhaps it is somewhat over-confident of me to be talking of mastering the great man's thought, but all I can do is make the attempt. The new Wittgenstein dictionary that I have purchased will be an invaluable aid in my endeavours.

7/8/98

I have just picked up the portrait of Wittgenstein that I had framed. I'm sure it will lend a touch of intellectual rigour to the atmosphere of my room. I am afraid however that I may have chosen the wrong frame. It does not seem to compliment the portrait at all, but instead gives it a heavy and somewhat lifeless feel. But I guess the picture itself is something of a despondent (very serious) view of Wittgenstein. It shows him to be quite an unhappy fellow. I have just as serious photos of him, but this one makes him look quite distraught with life. It was reputed to have lead a very unhappy existence, though his last dying words were, "let them know I've had a wonderful life." Sentiments I would assume most to want to utter at the end of a life. I will have to find out at what stage in Wittgenstein's life the photo was taken, to try and ascertain what dreadful thoughts may have been racing through his mind during the taking of it. I spent yesterday afternoon wandering around the grounds of the old exhibition buildings. The gardens there are not of the standard of the botanical, though they are pretty none the less. I'm glad I can once again enjoy such adventures, though not to the same intensity as I used to. Still I must be thankful for my new found wonder at the natural world. I have been contemplating going camping, though I think I am well and truly ensconced in my way of life here to contemplate a journey at the present. Perhaps some time in the future. I used to quite enjoy the outdoors and things such as camping, so I hopefully I will enjoy them again. Having talked to some of my friends, I have put thought to perhaps travelling overseas once again. If I did it would not be for some time, perhaps even a number of years, but the idea is still there. I was so young when I went to Europe the first time, I did not have the opportunity to fully appreciate the more sophisticated aspects of travelling. I could even in fact continue my studies overseas. That is, perhaps go to Cambridge and see were Wittgenstein lectured, and even go to Ireland and try and discover the cottage where he wrote some the *Philosophical Investigations*. Well they are just thoughts.

8/9/98

I have begun reading Homer's *Odyssey*. It's a book I have been meaning to read for quite some time. I am quite enjoying the story as it slowly unfolds. I also have the tale on an audio book format, though I think that I shall avoid availing myself of that means of immersing myself in the tale. To read is one of the greatest joys one can be given. I am developing a desire to go back and read all the great classic texts, to have at my disposal all those works that have inspired people throughout the ages. I shall have to once again explore the Greeks, Homer, Aeschylus and Sophocles and their ilk. Combine that desire with my Philosophical interests and I think I have booked up my reading time until the end of the year. I will have to have ago at reading some literature, something like Tolstoy or George Eliot, though my tastes have always been more inclined toward the classical. The same could be said of my taste in art, so I guess it could be said that I am something of a classicist. Philosophy is the only contemporary pursuit that seems to hold an interest for me. Modern literature and modern art seem to me not to posses the grandeur of the classical. I don't know whether this is an indictment against modern society, but all the modern masters don't to me seem imbued with the same visionary appeal as do those great masters of the by-gone eras. The art of the past maintains an elegance and grace which is rarely achieved in the modern. Perhaps Cezanne or Monet come about as close as a modern artists can get to the sublimity achieved by the great masters of the past. No one seems to have the gall to attempt those works which are on the grandest scale, those works attempting to achieve something truly great. I guess the great in fact lies in the mundane, well one can argue the case at any rate. So perhaps in their own way the modern artist is attempting to say something great. Of course I am generalising on quite a large scale here, but I think I am saying something of importance.

9/9/98

I am quite enjoying my reading of the *Odyssey*. My imagination is begging to come alive under the descriptive excellence of the story. The plight of Odysseus is truly one of great heroic adventure. His travels through the world of ancient Greece really do inspire one to perhaps go and see these parts of the world for oneself. I once studied under a lecturer who had travelled to Greece, and specifically those sites employed by the poets of that ancient time. His accounts of those places were inspiring in their vivid

Diary of a Schizophrenic

depictions. I think though if I travelled to Europe I would first visit those places made famous by the attendance of Wittgenstein, and then, and only then would I go searching further a field for other places of historical significance. But to see the ancient Greek sites would indeed be a treasure. To see the Oracle at Delphi, and the many outdoor auditoriums which the Greeks held there theatre within would be a joy. I never thought I'd enjoy the *Odyssey* as much as I have, but I guess it is one of the great classic stories, and has captured the imaginations of many a generations of readers. I think next I might attempt to read *Medea*. I once saw the play enacted, and really didn't enjoy the way Jason was portrayed. They depicted him as a very egotistical, almost tyrannical, figure. I found him much more heroic and noble. It is however a very fine line between the noble and egotistical. I guess it depends upon how one comes to view the text.

10/9/98

I have just completed a letter to my friend Edward Ellis. In it I ask him to pick a number of William Blake prints from a catalogue which has accompanied the letter, which we shall then view at the National Gallery of Victoria's prints and drawing department. I am quite looking forward to the excursion, for I have seen some these William Blake water colours and etchings before, and was quite impressed by them (of course). Blake had such visionary capacity. His watercolours capture the essence of the spiritual in their vivid display of colour. They are incredibly powerful, I find myself having difficulty viewing some of them, especially his watercolours of the *Inferno* by Dante. They seem imbued with some truth which Blake has seen and is conveying to the rest of the world. It is truly a shame that he did not complete the majority of the paintings in this series, for the ones which he did bring close to completion were very striking (to say the least). I think there power lies in their imaginative force, though it is an imagination which has seen things you or I have never seen, so in a sense is not purely imaginative. In fact I very much like the women which Blake depicts. They have a sensuality which is very classic in its portrayal. He gives the women which he paints and air of grace which draws its inspiration from the Greeks I think.

11/9/98

My reading of the *Odyssey* continues with great pleasure. The power of Homer's story telling abilities is quite remarkable. His eye for detail coupled with his vivid descriptive capacities combine to set the reader upon a wave of narrative euphoria. And the story telling runs so smoothly that one hardly notices that one is reading an epic story. It all comes very easily to the eye. I'm not sure if this is an effect of the translation into English, or if it is indeed a characteristic of the original text. Such fluidity in narration probably stems from the stories history as a piece of oratory. It really does strike one as being heard rather than being read - it just has that ease about it. The descriptions are not overly long winded, nor are they particularly concise. In describing the heroic manner of some particular character, there can be quite a vivid portrayal - while in describing a great tragedy that has just afflicted the crew of Odysseus' ship say, their can be quite scanty and skeletal descriptions. It all seems to depend upon where in the story an event is occurring. Odysseus' account of his own travels is imbued with just as much descriptive license as other parts of the story, though we are told that Odysseus is the master rhetoricist, and Homer makes it show very distinctly. Is Homer the greatest of the ancient story tellers? Who else might compare - Sophocles? Euripides? Aeschylus? Each have their unique capacities in relating a story, but I think none compare with the sheer epic quality of Homer. Each retell epic stories, but only Homer does so with such an eye for the grandeur of the epic. Which reminds me, that I should really go back and re-read some of those other dramatists, such as Sophocles or Aeschylus, though there are so many other things to read. I mustn't get overwhelmed buy the sheer number of things that I am attempting to read. Although I've got the next six months which I can entirely devote to whatever reading takes my interest.

Diary of a Schizophrenic

13/9/98

I have had the most remarkable improvement in the strength of my mind. For a brief hour I felt my mind regain its former potency - nay, even surpassing its former state. I could hardly believe what was happening. But unfortunately my newly found mind was not to last. I know how fragile newly formed minds can be, but recklessly I went into the bathroom and looked in the mirror to have a look at my new haircut. I was to pay a heavy price for that act of vanity. My mind immediately revert back to its old standing, in fact most of the gains I had made were taken away. The world has once again become like it had been. I feel this morning was a very important moment in my life, where the conditions were ripe for the strengthening of my mind. Who knows what could have eventuated in my life if I had not have been so vain as to look in that mirror. It must be the light reflecting from the glass which impinges itself upon my mind. It's the only explanation I can think of. Well never the less, I am left with only a portion of the mind which I had this morning. But oh what a joy it was to have regained my former mind. I could not have possibly dreamt of such a recovery. But as is usually the case, I come close to realising my dreams, only to have them taken from my grasp after only having experienced them for the briefest of times. I think of only how my life could have turned out if I had only attempted to stem my vanity. No, it was not entirely vanity, but curiosity at what my new haircut looked like. But I guess the majority of my life recently has been lived in regret for missed opportunities and things that have gone wrong. Despite all that has happened I still feel that I shall make a full recovery. The signs are good, all I need is a little bit of luck and for things to go my way. Ah, what an absolute joy it was to experience such a strengthened mind. But I guess it makes the tragedy of losing it that much harder to come to terms with. Still I live in hope of once again experiencing such a well strengthened mind.

Paul Fearne

14/9/98

I have yet again been set upon by the most unfortunate of circumstances. After obtaining a full recovery of my emotional capacities, I have succumbed to another harsh blow from fate. I am not sure if I have still retain the abilities to write. My mind has been dealt a very serious blow. I can't seem to construct complex sentences any longer. Where do I begin to try and explain how this feels? I am at wits end. My life has just passed before my eyes. All I did was turn on the computer, then quickly turn off. I then took a quick shave, and somehow the light reflecting from the mirror has destroyed my abilities to write coherently. I cannot believe it. My life is now over. I have to attempt to write something. There must be some way to avoid this fate! What are my views on Wittgenstein? What is my understanding of a language game? It seems to me that a language game is something of a modal unit of language use. There are a myriad of language games which constitute the whole range of uses to which language can be put. There is the language game of talking about the weather, the language game of mathematics, the language game of science. Also in the *Blue Book* Wittgenstein employs the term language game to refer to something primordial in the use of language. A language game is that which a young child plays when in the initial stages of language acquisition. The child assumes a role in determining the uses to which language can be put. There is the language game of learning new words and how they are employed within the larger context of the entire language. Well what about 'family resemblances'. Wittgenstein employs the concept family resemblance to tackle the problem which faces the philosopher when trying to determine the essence of language game. When one is looked for, that is when the essence of the concept of a language game is sought for, one cannot indeed be found. Rather there is a whole host a various interconnected and overlapping similarities in the various language games which, while providing the foundations upon which to call each a language game, do not constitute any essence which may be used to define the term language game. The same can be said of a whole host of other concepts. What about a

Diary of a Schizophrenic

'form of life'? This term plays a central role in Wittgenstein's later philosophy. While only appearing five times within the entirety of the *Philosophical Investigations*, it never the less commands a central place within any hierarchy of Wittgensteinian terms. And accordingly the concept is one of the most philosophically subtle and elusive which Wittgenstein employs. As with other Wittgensteinian concepts, the term 'form of life' is employed as therapeutic device, used to show the proverbial fly out of the fly bottle. A form of life is that shared by all members of a linguistic community. It constitutes the whole host of tacit presuppositions which go into forming the conditions under which a language is properly used. Actions, beliefs, tendencies, cultural and social imperatives are all constitutive of a form of life. People of differing cultures may in fact be said to maintain differing forms of life. For a stranger in strange lands has difficulty in finding his feet with the local language because the behavioural tendencies form the basis of language use are so very different from the one the traveller is used to. Also, not only are there cultural differentiations in forms of life, but also biological ones. A lion exhibits a differing form of life from the human, so it may be said that a "lion could speak we would not understand it". Wittgenstein is here making a comment about the basis upon which language rests. While weary of positing any thing which may be said to perform the role of an essence in language, the notion of a form of life is about as close as Wittgenstein gets to establishing one. It is the bedrock at which our spade is turned in our inquiries into such foundations. Well I think I will give it a rest there. I am still not entirely happy with the way my mind is functioning after the battering it has taken. My thoughts and ideas are not issuing from my mind with their usual clarity. I am having to struggle to put my ideas into words, in fact I am struggling even to have ideas. What was once a fertile bed of philosophical speculation, is now a barren landscape filled with dead carcasses of thought. I only hope that my mind can regain its clarity before I begin the research for my thesis. I am looking forward so much to writing it that I couldn't stand having anything coming in the way of its successful execution. Such dreams give my life a focus and a direction which is otherwise sorely lacking.

15/9/98

Well it's good to be at the computer after last night's drama. I really felt as though I had lost the ability to write. Though having the ability to write that long diatribe of philosophy gives me confidence that it's not the case. I really don't know what I would do if I happened to lose the ability to write. It would come as the most serious blow in the midst of a whole series of blows. But my mind seems always to be able to recover, which is good news. The vicissitudes which it must endure are indeed broad and diverse, but I remain hopeful that such hardships will be only temporary. I am at my happiest when I can write a short entry into my journal, and do a little bit of reading. My journey through the *Odyssey* continues, and I still quite enjoy it. I have reached the section where Odysseus returns to Ithaka disguised as beggar, and is sussing out the suitors who he intends to do battle with. I am looking forward to the confrontation, it should be quite an exciting affair. If the battle scenes from the *Iliad* are anything to go by, then the action should be quite fierce. Odysseus is renowned for his fighting prowess and should make quite a meal out of the suitors, though I will have to wait to find out exactly what happens. I am reading the *Odyssey* at quite a fast rate, about two chapters a day, so it shouldn't take me any time whatsoever to complete it. It lends a nice structure to my day, reading in the mornings, followed by an outing in the afternoon, followed by television in the evenings. I have to watch that I don't watch too much television though, although I quite enjoy watching the strong colours of some of the programs. Still, as they say, too much television is bad for you. It gives my days structure though, which is important. I can't read the entire day, so I have to do something to take my mind off things, just so I can relax. I'll just have to find something else which I can do which allows me time to relax. Although the television is the easiest and most readily available form of relaxation. And if I'm only watching a few hours a night, then it shouldn't be doing me that much harm.

Diary of a Schizophrenic

18/9/98

Well I have almost completed the *Odyssey*, and my, what an adventure it has been - the climactic scene! That hero Odysseus sure knows how to get violent. Or more to the point, I should say that Homer is the master at portraying violence in all its great and vivid detail. Odysseus returns to Ithaka to find a number of the local inhabitants courting his wife. It goes without saying that he is none to pleased and takes it upon himself to butcher every last one of them. The scene includes some of the most torrid violence that I have yet come across in literature - even rivalling a number of the scenes from the *Iliad*. The graphic detail is at times horrendous in its depiction of the bloody events. One does not know whether to marry ones sympathies with Odysseus or the hapless suitors, for they are indeed treated with the utmost contempt. But to the credit of the masterly Homer, one cannot help but be moved by the force of Odysseus' conviction, despite his violent ways. He is the hero returning triumphant to his long pined for homeland, bearing the spoils of war as well as the stories which accompany such exploits. His return is one of triumph, and there can be nothing which stands in the way of Odysseus' vengeance. It is a rightful vengeance, one imbued with the rites of savage yet honourable age. We care not for the marauding drunkards who have abused the privileges granted them under Odysseus' roof. And unlike the unfortunate Agamemnon, Odysseus has left a strongly faithful wife, who mourns her husband's departure, and continually delays the advances of the suitors for the duration of his absence. And it is her faith which must be rewarded by the deaths of those who have harassed her so unceasingly. In this modern age, one can never condone such violence, or the taking of justice into ones own hands. But such acts must be seen for what they are and in the context of the time in which they were enacted. For the story would simply lose its impact if the returning Odysseus was to let the suitors go with simple monetary restitution, as they had indeed suggested.

Paul Fearne

20/9/98

The world has seemingly come alive for me once again. I am able to "feel" the world, to experience the atmosphere of my surroundings - something which has been denied me for quite an extended period of time now. I am able to fully appreciate the grandeur of a summer day in a way that had become impossible for me. I don't believe there to be any words in the English language which help articulate what has recently transpired in my perceptual outlook. The world has once again come alive, where it had been dead and devoid of experiential substance. A summer can now feel like a summer, if one can catch my meaning. The smell of freshly cut grass, the feel of a balmy evening, the presence of warm air on one's skin, all these things, which seem so mundane and everyday, were denied me. But no more, I have them back with an intensity which is quite exhilarating. I don't know how I lived life without such experience. I guess now I am fully able to appreciate just what a blessing the simple experiences of a human life can be. All those things one takes for granted, the sights, the smells, the feelings, all have returned, and returned in abundance. I simply enjoy being outside, and immersing myself in the experiential play which surrounds me. Even simply going to the supermarket is something to look forward to, as it can yield a veritable treasure trove of new feelings and sensations. I went to Albert Park yesterday and was simply overcome buy the beauty of the place. It was a feeling I had not enjoyed perhaps since I went to America, it was the joy at seeing something new which exhilarates you. I had of course seen Albert Park many times before, but not for a long time had it seemed so beautiful and full of vitality. The moment was somewhat spoiled by my fear that my new found perceptual abilities would at any moment leave me. But my fear proved unfounded as I spent the day travelling though Melbourne just enjoying what I was seeing around me. The botanical gardens were also quite a treat. I felt like I was living an entire year ago.

Diary of a Schizophrenic

23/9/98

Something of a tragedy has just occurred in my life. The situation began quite harmlessly enough. I was playing with Charlie in the kitchen with the light off and I guess my eyes had become quite accustomed to the dim surroundings. All of sudden with no warning at all Colin come into the room and turned the light on. I had previously experienced such jumps from darkness to light, but never before with such intensity. You see the kitchen light is particularly bright and harsh on the eyes. My sensitive mind seems to be able to cope quite well with the extra intensity if it is only required to adjust from less light to more light, not from darkness to extreme light. At any rate the shock was quite tremendous, and I think my mind has been permanently damaged as a result. I seem to be writing quite fluently, so that part of my mind seems to have remained unscathed. There has been however a very terrible consequence of my exposure to such a brilliant light. There are times when my mind now behaves something like a broken record, and seems to get caught on certain thoughts, repeating them once or twice before moving on to the next thought. Also most thoughts incur something of an echoing effect - that is they are repeated in my mind before they meander of centre stage. It has become an almost maddening occurrence. I know not how long such a thing will last, or whether my mind has been permanently damaged. One consolation is there seems to be periods were such effects do not operate, particularly when I am doing things. Though it is those times in which I am unoccupied and just given to the act of thinking that the occurrence makes itself known most prominently. It is such a tragedy, as I was on the brink of making a full and uncompromising recovery. Life had once again become full of promise and the prospect of a bright future. My external world had come alive, and while it is still quite amazing, my enjoyment of it has been tarnished by the constant bewilderment I am caused by the state of my mind. I find solace in the fact that it was certainly some effect of karma that happened to find myself in that darkened room while Colin turned on the light. If that is the case then I have well and truly paid for any wrong I had engaged in during my past. Instead of emerging into a new world of wonder like I had been on the verge of doing, I am now forced to once again live in the these stark confines. I can only hope that such things do not have any permanent affects upon my mind.

26/9/98

Well this damnable blight upon my mind has yet to recede. I am quite fearful that the damage done may indeed be permanent. How can I describe the discomfort associated with this affliction? It is as if part of my mind was seared by the blinding light which I encountered upon that fateful day in the kitchen. As a broken record will get caught upon a particular phrase of a piece of music, so to my mind becomes stuck upon a certain thought, repeating that thought before moving on to the next thought. There are times when this occurrence is worse than others, so their are periods when I am able to gain some respite from the terrible discomfort which such an affliction maintains. I can only hope that my mind is somehow slowly repairing the damage. Every such instance of damage which has occurred in the past - and there have been none to this extent though - has not been of a permanent kind. My mind seems to recover at differing speeds depending upon the severity of the impingement. But close to a week as passed by, and I am yet to see any great improvement. I am thankful that my reading capacities have remained intact, though it is quite uncomfortable at times trying to think about the text I am reading while I am reading and while my mind continually catches on itself. Though such things are less noticeable while I am reading than at other times. I can't help but think about the remarkable recovery I would have made if only this had not happened. But as I have learnt only to well, the past is past and there is nothing which can bring back a single second of what's already happened. But I console myself with the fact that my other faculties, other than my thinking faculties, are all still intact. But so much of my life is spent in the act of thinking that I can hardly imagine a life under the reign of such a situation. There are periods in which I just enjoy spending lengthy periods thinking about my life and all the possibilities which it entails.

3/10/98

The tumult of the past week has receded into the past (for the time being at least). My mind has recovered from its linear character, and those recently occurred intrusions into my mental life seem to have taken flight. I can once again think without fear of some mental disturbance reeking havoc. I have begun reading Virgil's *Aeneid*. I am not quite enjoying it as much as the *Odyssey*, though it does have some saving graces. The story does not flow as smoothly and the plot is continually interrupted in its progress. As a result it is at times hard to follow the thread of the narration. Despite such flaws, which may indeed be a result of the particular translation which I am reading, there are moments of true genius within those ancient pages. The account given of the sacking of Troy is indeed vivid in its portrayal of events. The battle scenes are laced with a force of conviction that lends each description given something of living quality. It seems at times as if Virgil may actual have been there amongst the ramparts of Troy, witnessing the mighty battle as it unfolded. The intervention of the gods is an integral part of the story, and as with all accounts of divine intrusion into the human realm, one is left feeling awe struck at the power of such beings.

I am unhappy once again with my writing abilities. The flow of thoughts seems to have ceased somehow, and I am not articulating the few thoughts that I do have with any proficiency. My writing seems stilted and laboured, where it once had a certain flow and poise. I can feel something of a difference in the way my mind is formulating its ideas. I think I have once again had my mind damaged, this time by a shaft of light from the kitchen globe. I accidentally looked directly into the light this time, and I fear it has somehow damaged my mind. The thoughts are just not flowing as they once did.

4/9/98

I am wanting just to write a small paragraph to re-assure myself that my writing abilities are still with me. It just doesn't seem the same, there is no subtlety of thought present in the words I am typing. I read some of the material I composed a few weeks ago, and it maintains a definite strength - a certain force which impelled it to seek out new modes of expression. And my thinking now as I write is very laboured when compared to just a few short weeks ago. Yesterday, in describing my reactions to Virgil's *Aeneid*, I was very restricted in my use of vocabulary. It's as if that faculty concerned with the composition of complex sentential structures has become dormant - either through external infringement, or some internal whim of the mental. My guess is that yet again I have become the victim of some external vicissitudes which has compromised a part of my mind. This is a fear that I am forced to live with on a constant basis - the fear that my writing abilities, which are so dear to me, will eventually leave me, or lose their potency. To express oneself through the medium of the written word is very much the well-spring of my continued happiness in this world. I don't believe I am as proficient as I was say a year ago. But never the less, I still take immense pleasure in the articulation and expression of my thoughts. Even just the sensation of typing words into the keyboard is a source of pleasure. In fact, simply looking at my desk with the laptop nestled on top gives me a sense of pleasure. Such visual imaginings allow me to escape into a world of scholarly reflection, and give me a glimpse of a world that may have been - and who knows, may well still be. Just as long as my abilities as a writer do not depart. Well I feel somewhat relieved after having written these words. The thoughts are starting to flow once again, and while they are still a little stilted, I am happy with what I have produced. I guess one must endure such things.

7/9/98

Well my mother was down from Sydney this weekend and it is was great to see her again. She really seems to be enjoying life quite immensely at the moment, which is good to see. She has discovered a passion for astrology, and while it's not an interest which I harbour, one must still admire the force of her convictions. I remember when my passion were as virulent, but those times belong to a younger Paul Fearne, one on the cusp of adulthood who had the whole world before him. I'm sounding like an old man with those remarks, and I guess I feel old - well less innocent at any rate, after everything I've been through. An old school friend of mine dropped in to say hello this afternoon. It was also quite a treat catching up with him. Of course we went through what everyone was doing with their lives, and what we were doing with our own lives. Its always interesting to discover what your old school friends are up to. This particular friend of mine is working in the financial industry, which to me sounds like something of a tiresome occupation, but he seems to be enjoying it quite well. The whole office situation does not appeal to me in the slightest. One almost must feel a little sorry for those forced to endure such a life. Though I really haven't experienced such things, so it may well be a rewarding way to live - though of course my interests lay far a field. I still feel the world of academia holds much appeal for me. The hours of study and research suit me very amicably. Yes, the intellectual life would provide me with a suitably enjoyable occupation. I believe that is the direction which my brother wishes to take, so we may in fact both end up in the world of academia, which would be quite a turn of events. I enjoy my brother's company, he has a conversational ease which puts one at rest. I guess I enjoy being around people who talk a lot, because it allows me to recede into the background, just adding the occasional comment. I find I quickly get tired when forced to converse for extend periods. Though getting me talking about philosophy and it may well be a different situation. Though just recently I haven't really had the opportunity to really have such a conversation. But I'm sure that will come once I've begun my honours year.

10/9/98

A friend of mine from high school called this afternoon. It was quite a treat talking with him once again, for we only rarely talk. And he said something to me which really struck a nerve. He made a comment to the effect that, when next we should meet, we should talk of life, the universe, and everything. Now he was making comment on my old tendency toward speculative thought, my inquiring mind which took delight in all things universal. And it occurred to me that I have totally forgotten what I used to be like, before my innocence was so rudely snatched away. I was a deep thinker, one concerned with all the larger questions of life - a philosopher one might say. Deeply interested in religion and in coming to some fuller appreciation of what life was about. It has never occurred to me just to what extent these last two years have taken from me. Such thoughts are now far from my mind, and the meaning of life rarely occupies my thinking. What was once a wonderfully rich bank of inspiration and material upon which to reflect, has dried to become a barren creek bed. Life no longer holds that wonder for me as it once had. I merely survive, from one day to the next. I have my routines, and they keep me occupied - they keep one day flowing to the next. But it is just simply survival, nothing more. I believe I was destined for a richer life than the sterile one which I now lead. My emotions were my well-spring. They were at times very intense, but they provided me with moments of wonderful elation. But these things are now only memories, and are only vaguely remembered ones at that. I now must endure a life of bland acceptance of my lot in life, with little hope of recapturing what once was mine. This must be what a person of greater vintage must feel like, that all the best days of ones life were now well and truly behind one, and that now there is only the long wait for the immanence of death. But that for me is so far off, and there is still so much of life to go for me, that it seems hardly fair. Well there is still hope, but nowadays that's a thing I hardly feel, though it is still there.

Diary of a Schizophrenic

4/1/99

I write this journal entry, and those to follow, with the explicit intention of improving the execution of my English. A journal, of course, has a myriad of other useful functions. Indeed, I am in no doubt that the regular upkeep of such a record will provide the fertile soil from which many new ideas and insightful reflections will spring. Not only will I keep account of my daily business, but I also hope to furnish the following pages with thoughts concerning my chosen areas of study, and perhaps even inspirations for poems and novels. But overriding all these considerations is an earnest desire to improve in some marked degree my grasp of the English language. To this end I may even attempt some form of linguistic experimentation, with regards to grammar, expression and explication – all for the sole purpose of coming to a deeper understanding of the my native tongue. The last few weeks have seen my plans for the future start to take shape, and almost all of the options upon which I am staking a claim involve writing. It is writing, in some form or other, that I am determined to make my vocation in life. Wether it be in the realms of academia, secondary school teaching, or as a professional writer penning considered words of much esteem. Whichever path beckons the surest and gains my undying devotion, I am in urgent need of precise and unencumbered command of the English language. The language faculty of the human species is perhaps the most important of all the faculties – for a firm grasp upon the tenets of language allows one not only to express more complex thoughts and emotions, but also to *experience* new thoughts and emotions that would have otherwise remained unknown. A person's realm of experience is actually enhanced with a larger vocabulary and firmer understanding of the workings of language. Without the correct language tools, one is consigned to an abyss of experiential deprivation. Language is the mirror which reflects the world, and if your mirror is cloudy then you will surely perceive an indistinct image. Problems dissipate when one is able to consider a quandary from the vantage of an increased precession of vocabulary and grammar. These are bold claims which never the less are shown as true by the world at large. Those with a surer understanding of language will achieve to greater levels, for all facets of life are conditioned by how one is able to express oneself to the world.

6/1/99

I am finding that my days are becoming inordinately busy. I have only been back in Melbourne for five days, and already I am overwhelmed with things to do. I don't even seem to have the time to begin my study regime, though I have found one afternoon in which I buried myself within the confines of the Gibson Library. It's been so long since I have been so busy. I am however thrilled that my life has so suddenly become full of things needing to be achieved. And amongst all the commotion I have found the opportunity to spend time with friends, something I have been guilty of neglecting in the past. It seems that my recent trip to Europe has proved me with a certain momentum which has propelled into the blazing heat of life without so much as a peaked cap. I guess I've just realised just how much I wish to achieve and just how many things that I wish to occupy my time with. There are my scholarly interests, my passion for literature and poetry, my enjoyment of music, my love of the theatre and all the art forms, my fondness for the outdoors and my desire to gain a strong command of the English language. Each pursuit has begun placing its own demands upon my time, and I'm finding it difficult to undertake everything. Most of my time must be spent preparing for the upcoming year of study, but my evenings are still free to do as I please. But never the less they are becoming cluttered. It seems I will simply have to go to bed later and rise earlier. As of late I've been sleeping about twelve hours a day – but I fear I must say goodbye to those days and embrace a temporally stricter regime. My plans are to go to bed about 11pm and arise about 8am. This should allow me time to devote to my pursuits. I also have much to write about. I plan to enter into a full review of my travels and write of my impressions of

Diary of a Schizophrenic

the poetry I have recently been reading. This of course must come amidst the hurly-burly of the recording of my daily goings-on. But I shall wait for tomorrow to embark upon such a noble quest.

7/1/99

I think its due time to embark upon a review of my European adventure, and reflect upon the multifarious impressions which I had during those travels. I certainly got a lot more out of my travels through Europe this time, but I simply put that down to the maturation process. I was painfully young when I first visited Europe, and to say nothing else my knowledge of European culture (literature, art & history) was vastly inferior at that time in my life. With a more intimate understanding of such things on this occasion I was able to better appreciate the cultural heritage of the countries to which I sojourned. The visiting of art galleries, museums and libraries occupied most of my time, and their influence upon which quite pronounced. With some knowledge of European art I was able to allow myself those feeling of awe struck amazement one experiences when viewing a work which has previously only been seen in the confines of an art book. Renoir's *La Loge* was a superb highlight in such respects. The image had moved me from the printed page and did not fail to do so from the canvas. There were other works, Leonardo da Vicini's *Virgin of the Rocks*, Ingress's *Turkish Bathers*, and of course not forgetting the William Blake collection at the Tate. Though of course I was quite disappointed to find the *Pity, Like a Newborn Babe* was not being shown. I was more than adequately compensated however when the curators of the Fitzwilliam Museum allowed me the privilege of viewing Blake's *The Marriage of Heaven and Hell*. The colours were striking in their intensity, and Blake's attention to the minuetest detail left me astounded. I had no option but to send the curator a letter of my sincere thanks for giving such a sensory feast. It was perhaps one of the most beautiful things I have seen. The facsimile editions just cannot do justice to the original work – in colour or detail. And what's more I was allowed to read the entire manuscript. So in fact I read the work just as William Blake had intended it to be read. But there is much more to tell of, but I will wait until tomorrow to continue my reflections.

8/1/98

I am afraid I have to postpone the recording of my impressions of Europe. A more pressing matter demands my attention. I have just discovered that, contrary to my initial understandings, I have not after all complete a major in English as part of my degree. I have obtained an honours entry level in the subjects which I have completed, but have not undertaken the required number of subjects to qualify me for a major in English. This comes as enormous blow to aspiration for the future. I had envisioned either a scholarly career in the English faculty, a position as a secondary school teaching English, or as a professional writer. All these plan are now cast into uncertainty. My one remaining hope is that I may somehow undertake a number of additional English subjects to bolster my enrolment and thereby qualify for postgraduate study in English. It is the weekend now, so I will have to wait for the week to begin anew before I can discover what my options may possibly be. Of course my options in the philosophy department are still open, though I have to say my passion is being channelled into the fields of literature, and I am starting to believe that this is where my destiny lies. I have lost that fertile bed of thoughts and ideas which has sustained me in my philosophical studies, though I am still quite interested in the field. But I have a far more in depth knowledge of literature than I do of philosophy, and most of my spare to is diverted into reading in that area of interest. I am at a loss what to do. This situation could shape the rest of my life if nothing can be done. But I am hopefully the English department has measures in place to accommodate students such as myself who have recently become swept away with an enthusiasm for literature. I am sure if I can just be afforded the opportunity to state my case then allowances can be made for me. For all I want to do is write. Of course I can write in the field of philosophy, but I am

Diary of a Schizophrenic

finding my natural affinity is toward all endeavours in the English department. I am of course more familiar with the philosophy department, for I have spent a good deal of my time there over the course of my degree. I guess it has only been a recent shift in my loves, from philosophy to English, but I really feel this may be the direction in which I wish to shape my life.

9/1/99

I have just enjoyed an exceedingly pleasant evening. An old friend of mine came by to pay me a visit. He was accompanied by his wife, and the two of them were indeed very charming. Our conversation traversed such wide and fertile fields that it was simply a joy to be present. Peter spoke of his love for music, and myself for my passion for poetry and literature. We exchanged thoughts on such varied topics as the structure of the creative process, the intricacies of the married life, and the psychological impact of early-life events. Peter is truly a man of great heart and does in some marked degree epitomise the soul of the artistic temperament. He is not a man who suffers for his art, though this is not to say that he does not immerse his whole being in the pursuit of artistic purity. He has in many respects overcome those troubled anxieties which did so plague his younger years, and the dreaded tendrils of melancholy have long been banished to the vault of remembrance. There is in him not the slightest untoward tendency; he is a soul of composed and considered optimism who thrives upon the winds of charity. His unquestionable command of all things musical is perhaps the well-spring which sustains his life; giving it shape and reason. There is no denying the true talent which is his beloved possession, a gift which will provide him sure passage to the harbour of fame, in my considered opinion. Creative genius takes many forms, but is often accompanied by the most sublime aspects of humanity; industry, fortitude, compassion, and generosity to name but a few of the arrows shot by nature's bow. And Peter maintains all these and more. His constitution is in not the slightest degree bereft of any of these traits; indeed it does exemplify them to the last. To say nothing more, it was a joy to share in his company and partake of his conversation.

10/1/99

My life seems to be forming itself into a tightly compacted whole. I mean by this that my daily activities are filling my mornings, afternoons and evenings; leaving no idle time whatsoever. This is not to say that I have no time to spend on leisure, quite the contrary. In fact I spent today at the National Gallery of Victoria and wandering through the delightful spaces of the botanical gardens. I could not have asked for a more pleasant afternoon. What I mean is that I'm always finding myself with things to do. There is no time for the constrictive clutches of boredom to wrap themselves around my life. I guess it's fair to say that I rarely feel boredom, in fact I'd say I never feel it. But never the less, if I did there would be no time to let it envelop my life. There is simply too much to read, listen to and write about that I can barely stand the thought of wasting a single moment in idle disinterest. This is not to say that one can't relax in some mindless pursuit – like watching television for instance. But I am finding that the unholy tube is only demanding an hour of my time per day, though I enjoy watching a movie on the weekends. But the movies which I hire are always thought provoking and informative, so they really can't be classified as mindless. So I guess what I'm trying to say is that I'm coming to feel something of a glow of satisfaction about how my life is proceeding. The future still beckons with sweet enticements, the past rarely occupies my mind, and the present is filled with industrious pursuits and noble pass times. So there really is little more that I could ask for at the moment. Well perhaps a girl friend would lend some form of icing to this already tasty cake. But I've been so long without one that I have grown accustomed to life as a busy single male. There is never the less something to be said for sharing your life with someone; your hopes, dreams and aspirations. And of course there's sex. Not forgetting that for a single moment. But all in all I'm quite satisfied with how my life is progressing that I'm not sure that there is any room

Diary of a Schizophrenic

for a girlfriend. No this is quite silly, I'm sure I could always find room for someone in my life. It's just a matter of finding the right person. And I don't really have a large circle of friends through which to meet someone, well not someone who I would be interested in at any rate.

11/1/98

Well the details of my academic progress are beginning to clarify themselves. What I thought was a hopeless situation has turned out to be quite harmless. I am still able to complete a major in English simply by overloading for a semester – that is to say over-enrol in two extra subjects beyond the number of points which it would usually take to complete my degree. The only implications of such a move will be that I must postpone my honours year – commencing it mid-year instead of at the start of the year. This will allow me a semester to complete the two subjects which I require to complete the English component of a double major. When it was finally discovered that I could after all complete my English major I was overcome with the most peculiar feeling. It was a yearning to do philosophy. Strange as this sounds (after my heart-felt pronouncements of a few days ago), the thought of postponing my honours year in philosophy left me somewhat despondent. It seems as if the thought of doing philosophy still after all holds some appeal for me. But never the less, I am thinking that I will undertake these two overloaded English subjects. It just opens to many doors for me to disregard it as an option. By simply doing straight philosophy I am locked into a career in academy in that department. And while I haven't entirely ruled that out, there are other things which I may well wish to do. I am most definitely considering a career in academia, though that my well be in the English department rather than the philosophy. And also, if my academic aspirations aren't fulfilled, I must consider secondary school teaching as an option. And if that is the case, then I could only see myself teaching English. The avenues which are opened in secondary teaching to the student who has only studied philosophy are quite limited, and there doesn't seem to be anything in that domain which particularly takes my fancy. So all things considered, to invest the extra six months in completing two additional English subjects seems the sensible thing to do. The only problem which may eventuate is that the person who may well be supervising honours thesis is retiring at the end of the year, and so may not be around to guide me in the final six months of that endeavour. The philosophy department has been stricken with a shortage of academic staff, so there might not be anyone else is able to supervise my efforts. But I will talk to Dr. Simone Collins, the philosophy honours co-ordinator, tomorrow and determine whether there is any one else who is willing and able to supervise me. But this being the only the concern, I think I will decide to undertake the extra semester of overloaded study. This is however subject to the approval of the arts faculty, so I am hoping that they will be sympathetic to my plight and allow me to overload during the upcoming semester. I think a carefully worded letter to the right person may well lubricate the administrative cogs so as to ensure that I undertake such a course of action.

12/1/98

The more I delve into the misty recesses of the English department, the more I am displeased with what I find there. I am alienated from the agendas which are being touted, and without cause to think otherwise, I am in general disheartened by the way certain texts are being crucified on the cross of intellectualism. Maybe it is that I should content myself with simple enjoyment of a text, rather than seek a heightened knowledge of the subtleties contained in the broader context of a work. I feel I am opposed to the over-intellectualisation of a text, and yet this is the seasoned domain of the English department. Perhaps I am being unfair, and should really suspend my judgement upon such matters until I have undertaken a few additional forays into such matters. But I think as far as my academic progress is concerned, I will follow my interest in philosophy, and see where that may lead. I feel more "at home" in the philosophy department. I know the people there, I am comfortable studying in the philosophy library, and I think my writing skills are more attuned to expression of philosophical argumentation. The only point of discontent is that I sometimes find the subject matter of philosophy very dry and at times misdirected. I have a greater knowledge of literature than I do of philosophy, and in the main there are very few philosophers who can hold my interest. The history of literature is to me a more fertile bed of inspiration than is the history of philosophy. So it seems that I am enamoured by the subject matter of English, but feel lost in the departmental labyrinth, and am disinterested in a great deal of the subject matter of philosophy, but feel more at home in the department. What a predicament! I'm sure I will find, both with a greater knowledge of philosophy, and a greater familiarity with the English department, that both bridges will eventually be crossed. Where does that leave me now then? Well I feel that I will do the extra two subjects in English, simply because that allows me greater flexibility to shape my future, and opens to many doors for me to disregard.

13/1/99

I think I shall leave the turmoil surrounding my academic planning and recommence the review of my travels to Europe. I have thought long and hard over the question of whether travelling actually changes you in some fundamental way. Whether one's views and opinions differ in some marked degree as a result of having travelled. I don't feel that travelling changes a person that extensively. It rather allows one to sample cultures of diverse ethnological and political constitutions, which would otherwise remain unknown. Such exposure to other cultures can in fact nurture a heightened awareness of one's own culture through allowing the traveller a view of such cultures from the outside. The traveller becomes aware of the idiosyncrasies apparent within his or her own set of culturally orientated behavioural dispositions. Through a comparison of how a foreign people conduct their lives to that of the traveller's native peer group, there results a more thorough appreciation of the complexities inherent within the original cultural network. I don't believe that one person can ever truly understand another. Even people of similar ethnic backgrounds. This is not to say, however, that *some* degree of understanding can be achieved. Indeed this is the very essence of the travelling experience. To come to know the English as reserved or the French conversational, is to begin to know the cultural stereotypes of one's own country of origin, and to begin to see them as in many ways false, or at least limited. Travelling allows one to develop a tolerance of different ways of life. To find one self as a foreigner in a strange land with little understanding of the native tongue is to suddenly feel a deep affinity with all minority groups within a society. And through such an awakening, there is an assimilation of prejudices; a process that allows for the final elimination of such tendencies form a person's tacit behavioural make up.

14/1/99

I have of late developed quite a passion for the romantic poets. Blake, of course, has been for some time now been the most favoured of poets. The sheer vitality of his imagination is enough to sustain his poetry through the most scrupulous criticism. What he lacks in technical merit is balanced by the weight of his convictions and the intensity of his imaginative faculties. That one needs a specialised dictionary to come to terms with some of his epic poetry is in no way an indictment of his prowess as a poet. In fact such symbolic complexity is a sign of a mature and achieved poet. The depth of psychological insight that Blake instils in his works can only be fully realised through the use of a heightened complexity of symbolic representation. The drama which is enacted between the main protagonists of the poems is itself a highly stylised and symbolic form of psychological analysis. To understand what Blake is trying to achieve it is necessary to let his symbolism work its way with your subconscious. There are times when one must relinquish ones sure grip upon life's mundane reality, and embrace the transforming flames of Blake's prophetic program - in all its spiritual fervour. Leave the rationalising mind at the first word you read, and rather step out into the poetry as a newborn babe taking its first steps. At first there is difficulty, but given some familiarity and practice there comes accomplished determination. And with that follows steadfast mastery of the chosen pursuit. So while Blake might be difficult, notoriously so, the rewards encumbered by a diligent analysis of his poetry are nothing short of deeply satisfying. And to then appreciate the artistic merit inherent in Blake's illustrated designs is nothing short of the icing of the cake. His art lends nothing but clarity to his sometimes obscure work. Such clarity does not come at the expense of refined complexity, for there is ample expressive conviction in Blake's artistic vigour. Just as he admonishes his readers in the preface to one of his epic poems, one must love him for the passionate execution of his work, even if the practical details are somewhat uncertain. But even to take Blake on his own word here is to suffer him a grave injustice. For his genius demands the full attention of ever aspect of his poetry.

15/1/99

Well everything has eventuated particularly well in regard to my studies. It turns out that I have after all completed a major in English and have indeed qualified for entry into honours. This means that I can now enrol in a combined honours year in both English and philosophy. I couldn't be happier. Both my passion and my talent are now appeased. I can now postpone a decision on the direction that my postgraduate studies will take until the end of the year. At the moment I am inclined to take up further studies in the English department. Simply because this is where my passion now lies. But I must not forget my capacity to understand and propound philosophical argumentation. It has held me in good steed over the course of my degree, and it would be a shame to relinquish my philosophy studies so soon. But one must follow one's heart, and I find that all my spare time is consumed with reading in the fields of poetry and literature. I am sure that I shall vacillate throughout the year, so I will postpone a final decision until the completion of my honours year. Today I read through two of my old English essays, both written on Blake. They showed remarkable poise and scholarly acumen. Reading them inspired me to consider writing my thesis in the English department. Though I still think I should not squander the work I have already placed in the planning of my philosophy thesis. I have quite a sound grasp of the technicalities of Wittgenstein's notion of a 'form of life'. And although it is quite a subtle and at times difficult concept to articulate philosophically, I feel I have come to a strong understanding of the concept as it is contextualised in the *Philosophical Investigations*. One thing which the recent crisis in my enrolment has done, is to realise from the mists the directions in which my life might take. I have been forced to think long and hard over the implications of my preferred endeavours. But I think I'm coming to realise that my dreams of entering into academia may well be realised, given of course a successful year this year. And even if such aspirations do not eventuate, then I have a number of secondary avenues which I may take. There is the option of secondary school teaching or even professional writing.

16/1/98

For about a week now I have been reading Milton's *Paradise Lost* in the evenings before I retire. Even after having read Shakespeare I could hardly have imagined a more dynamic use of the English Language. Milton still must play second fiddle to Shakespeare on my account though. Shakespeare imbues deeper psychological insight into his works, and is not as bound by the things which influence him. Never the less, *Paradise Lost* is a phenomenal excursion into the realms of poetic genius. The metaphor, figures and conceits which Milton employs are clad in such mastery of the language they simply leave one amazed. Some of the speeches given by Satan are beyond measure in history of literature. In Milton's attempts to convey the sublime he has left no mount un-scaled in terms of rhetorical precision. And there is present in *Paradise Lost* the most remarkable rhythm. The words ebb and flow in a veritable symphony of linguistic expression. One is swept along by this rhythm, unable to escape even if one tried. For to read the work is to participate in an act of imaginative creation. The subject matter of the work materialises in the consciousness of the reader, unmediated by the usual boundaries which constrain the written word. Milton has written something which not only appeases the intellect, but also engages the heart. We are shocked at the battle amongst heaven's occupants, enraged by Satan's audacity, enamoured by the innocence of the original inhabitants of earth, and feel pity at their plight. It is such an ambitious thing which Milton has attempted, it consoles us all the more that he has succeeded in his endeavours. And I am still yet to turn the final page! I wait in anticipation to read the crescendo described in the fall of Adam and Eve from paradise.

17/1/99

I have just spent an evening with my old secondary school English teacher. I was invited to dinner at her new home in Williamstown. The apartment has gorgeous views of Melbourne's CBD and is situated in the midst of one of the up and coming suburbs. The apartment itself is perched atop an old bank on the main shopping street of Williamstown. It dates architecturally from around the turn of the century. The façade has been modified for use in the 1990's, with more window space being added, and an extension has been undertaken on the right hand side of the building. A scuba-diving shop now inhabits the downstairs space, while the apartment is situated on the second level. The interior has been thoroughly modernised and refurbished, and the backyard contains a carport and a swimming pool. The evening was indeed a pleasant one, though I am afraid that I was not at my best. The conversation was stimulating to say the least, for Carmel's daughter has just completed her honours year in anthropology, so the discussion skirted all things academic. But I simply was not at my conversational best. I usually am quite interesting and charming in a more intimate setting, though I found myself trying to hard to impress in the presence of my old mentor. I quite like Emily, Carmel's daughter. Her manner was exuberant and her obvious intelligence was a delight to be in the presence of. But again I found I was very laboured in my conversations with her. I'm certain that we would have much in common, and that our passions would intersect. I think I became just a little nervous in the presence of such an attractive and intelligent woman. One thing which this evening has done for me is to steel my resolve to become a writer. Whether of fiction or non-fiction, scholarly or professional, I need the stimulus which writing provides to give my life coherent meaning. I need to be able to express myself in the written medium in order to live a full and complete life. There were times during the evening when all I could think about was writing. Increasingly such thoughts are occupying my mind.

18/1/99

Well I've finally decided to write my thesis in philosophy. I have a sound understanding of the topic which I plan to write upon, and even find myself experience a level of insight into the details involved. I decided to take a rest this afternoon in a park just near the university, and proceeded to lay down on one of seats. It must have been the peaceful surrounds, for I found myself reflecting at some length upon things philosophical. It felt good to be once again exercising my mind in the field of philosophy. Though I feel I have lost some of the intensity of the philosophical insights of my youth, there still seems to be a certain clarity involved in my thoughts on such matters these days. I thrive on the moments where my mind becomes clear as to philosophical puzzlement. It's quite exhilarating. Unfortunately as of late those moments have been few and far between. Maybe it is a direct result of my busier life style. Perhaps I need to give myself time to nurture such thoughts and encourage them to bloom. A more frequent occurrence of such insight will no doubt serve to enhance my success during the up coming year. But I can just wait and see. I find myself a little behind schedule due to the distractions caused by the changing of my enrolment. Though now that I am clear upon what I will write upon, there shouldn't be much trouble in concentrating my efforts once again. I plan to arise at about eight and get the day underway as soon as possible. This has proved very difficult as of late, for my habitual sleeping patterns demand that I sleep at least 12 hours a night. It is however just a matter of habit, and I am sure that once I have conditioned myself to sleep for only eight hours, then I will be fine. I must prepare myself for the onslaught which is the workload in an honours year. I have been warned by a number of people what to expect. So it's a shame I haven't been able to work consistently through January, but I will ensure that matters are rectified before the beginning of term.

19/1/98

My good friend Jill Garner has just arrived home from a brief interlude in Europe. She seemed quite vibrant over the phone, and so I must conjecture that she enjoyed herself. Well, you really must be something of a dill not to enjoy yourself in Europe. Though having said this, she did spend a period of approximately two weeks in Athens, and her report of the Greek culture left much to be desired. She told of her first ever experience of culture shock (she has travelled to Europe previously and suffered no such discomfort). The entire way of life exhibited by the Greeks left her feeling dismayed. I must say, I has not much enamoured by Athens, but the trip to the Greek islands more than made up for any displeasure I may have felt there. But it is true; being a foreigner in Greece does make one feel like just a mere commodity in the tourism vortex. A piece of meat as it were, ready to be sold to the highest bidder. But despite this abhorrence felt toward the ancient city of Athens, the rest of her trip proceeded quite amicably. But it is good the have her back. I was beginning to feel the weight of the world upon my shoulders, but a brief conversation with her has restored my faith in humanity. I shall have lunch with her tomorrow and we will no doubt discuss at some length the details of her travels. I have quite a busy weekend ahead, with two functions that I must attend. I find my life developing into a nice rhythm, with my work and social life being harmoniously balanced. My weekends are occupied with friends, while my weekdays are dedicated to study. I must prepare for a ferociously busy year, so the earlier I can get started, the more prosperous will be my final results. I really do enjoy the studying life style. Spending one's day in a library is such a pleasant way to exist. And the university grounds are so beautiful, that it really makes for a wonderful experience. I would not have it any other way.

20/1/98

I'm afraid life doesn't get much better than this. The day began with a short period of reading the newspaper. After I had read my fill, I took up the philosophical texts and commenced a short study session. I was forced to conduct the session at home, for I was waiting upon a phone call form my friend Jill. The call came around 11.20am. We organised to meet for lunch at approximately 1pm. In the interim another friend called. This time it was Christine Alexander. I hadn't seen her for some time so we arranged to meet for coffee in the afternoon around 4pm. Now I am rarely so social, but I have made it one of my resolutions to be a little more socially active. So after paying my university fees I made my way down to Droul's café to have lunch with Jill. Our relationship continued as if she hadn't been away a day. Our topic of conversation broached a multitude of topics, and it was truly a joy to engage so thoughtfully with another human being. The conversation sallied back and forth with great expressive ardour, and we finally ended up talking for something in the order of two and a half hours. But so immersed was I in the conversation that its duration seemed no more than an hour. After saying good-bye to Jill, I made my way to Brighton to have coffee with Christine. And again the conversation was interesting and provocative to say the least. I had purchased a gift for her while overseas, so I proceed to give it to her. She was thoroughly pleased to have received a copy of an edition of the collected shorter plays of Samuel Beckett – one of her favourite dramatists as it turns out. At any rate, we sat in a café in the main shopping street of Brighton for about an hour. When then proceeded to take a walk along the local beach. We again sat and continued to talk for about an hour and a half. Once again the conversation travelled far a field, though the writing process was one conversational sanctuary which sustained our attention. The afternoon ended with a pleasant drive back to North Melbourne with the radio tuned to a classical station. Then, after arriving home, I proceeded to watch the Philoppousis versus Chang tennis match on the television. I rarely get emotional while watching a sporting event, but I have to say I choked back the tears after Philoppusis' stirring victory. The five set match had everything, and it was a joy to watch. By this time it was about 8.25pm, so I thought I'd better get something to eat. So I ordered a pizza to be picked up from the local Italian restaurant. The actual walk to the restaurant was pristine. The sun had just set and a fiery red hue had light up the sky. It was that special time when day becomes night, and there is a certain stillness in the air. Needless to say I thoroughly enjoyed my walk. The pizza was fine, just large enough to satisfy me without being to large so as to make me over full. Well, that was my day. And I have to say it was one of the most splendid I have enjoyed for some time.

21/1/99

I just had the pleasure of driving my brother to the local video library. I always enjoy doing little errands like that for him. We usually end up talking at some length about the topics of the day, for he is quite a voracious news watcher. He has really matured into an out-standing young man who takes life for what it is. There's neither fuss nor bother in his demure. Things rarely trouble him to any large extent, and so he is at most times in a state of hyper-extended relaxation. Science is his chosen discipline of study, though he is doing a double degree with the arts faculty. In fact his best results have been in the philosophy department, so he maintains a decided talent in the arena of arts. He rarely allows life to become too complex, and so leads quite an untroubled existence. His wife Sophie is the perfect foil for his personality, and the two of them make an excellent match. She is quite a talented young lady with an aptitude for languages. She is also doing a double degree in science and arts, so has a diversity of talents. She plays a number of musical instruments, including the cello, the piano and the recorder. Like William she has undeniable conversational capacity which she employs toward making one feel extremely comfortable. Her manner is confident and assured, while her intelligence is self evident. Together they lead a life of tranquil acceptance. Sophie is the more social of the two and is often found with friends. They have a nice modern apartment just of Lygon Street with easy access to the university. Their home his filled with the latest appliances and home entertainment devices, and is quite well furnished with fashionable tables and chairs.

24/1/99

Amazing! I made it a resolution to indulge a little more frequently in social interaction, but nothing could prepare me for the sublimation of my existence caused by the recent escalation in the amount of time I have spent with friends. I am socially exhausted. For a person who sustains his life through the medium of solitary pursuits, it has meant a re-evaluation of my self-conceptions. I am sure, however, that this recent increase in my social interaction is just the crest of wave that will soon break, leaving me to sun my self upon the beach of solitary contentment. Never the less, I have had quite a fantastic time. I have found buried deep within my being a newly found comfort in the presence of others. Whereas previously there was only found pain and discomfort in social interaction, there is now a weighty confidence that imbues my social discourse with ease and maturity. I did meet on Friday night a very special lady indeed. It was a birthday function for a mutual friend, and from the first I knew that I would want to meet her. Rarely however does a meeting proceed so effortless. We were introduced and it became apparent that we were both students of the University of Melbourne. But the repour that we were to develop did not rest solely on this particular common ground. Our conversation roved far a field, extending its range over a diverse and stimulating set of topics. I immediately felt at ease in her presence, and felt assured that my comments would be received in interested consideration, while her comments where nothing short of insightful and intellectually pristine. We talked of travel, poetry, Russian literature, the contemporary state of the classics and many other things, to numerous to mention. It happens that she is an editor on the team at *Farrago*, which immediately impressed me. She implored that I submit something for the upcoming issue, and in all possibility I may do just that. But I shan't forget her warm demur and sharp intellect. A combination which is rarely found. I hope to see her relatively soon, so that we may continue in a similar fashion to our first meeting.

25/1/99

I have begun reading Walt Whitman's *Leaves of Grass*. Now there is a poet who revels in the divinity of humanity. Whitman is uncompromising in his insistence that the human condition is the wellspring from which all that is great and powerful in the world emerges. His portrayal of the everyday is instilled with a noble sentimentality that pervades his poetic work. The romantics wrote poems in a similar vein, although Whitman can in no way be compared to these poets. Writing in free verse, Whitman's poems convey the unconventionality of the soul through the medium of an uninhibited symphonic narrative. The dressmaker, the tailor and the seamstress take centre stage in Whitman's human drama, revelling in the blissful mundanity of their lives. No other poet, expect perhaps Blake, expresses such accomplished confidence in the supremacy of the human soul. Like Milton, Whitman attempts to convey the sublime through his poetic voice. Unlike Milton, however, Whitman uses the language of the common person. This in no way limits the range and depth of Whitman poetical struggle; it only enhances the triumphant victory which ensues from such a remarkable poetic aptitude. Blake pushed the boundaries of language in his attempts to raise the perceptions of humanity toward a glimpse of the eternal, and Whitman in a similar vain struggles at time to convey the intensity of the insights he had gained. But as T. S. Eliot wrote "...Words strain/ Crack and sometimes break, under the burden/Under the tension, slip, slide, perish,/Decay with imprecision..." I am certain that he to come upon the limits of language in his endeavours to describe what he saw. But it is a mark of their achievements that they could still muse upon the inarticulate in such bold poetic strokes. Whitman truly takes his place within the centre of the American canon.

26/1/98

What is it about the theatre that so invigorates the soul? Is it some voyeuristic tendency on our part that we need to be privy to the lives of fictional characters to forget our own concerns? Of course people enjoy discussing the lives of others. Is this some clue or an unrelated idiosyncrasy? Maybe it something a little more fundamental. One could say that a play reflects the prevailing moods and preconceptions of the day, though this fails to explain the interest levied in drama from other cultures and time periods. Aristotle defined drama as engaging in a certain *mimesis*, or imitation of life. Human beings take pleasure in viewing a cultural production that reflects something inherently similar in their own condition. Drama of different cultures can trade in the currency of a common humanity, and so still play upon the emotive responses of an international audience. For me personally, the theatre represents a cathartic experience which, in certain circumstances, can precipitate a fundamental awareness of my emotive faculties. Emotions, intense, unremitting emotions are what the theatre is all about. To be moved by the plight of a character, to sympathise and feel the vicissitudes of un-fortuitous fate. If a play can evoke a certain range of emotions then it is a success. But there seems something more to it than this. There can be a pure aesthetic appreciation of the playwright's skill and in the language which imbues the play. Such an aesthetic sense is perhaps reserved for those who maintain a certain level of dramatic knowledge, and doesn't seem to explain the fundamental appeal which a play can extend upon an audience of varying familiarity with the various dramatic forms. There is indeed something primeval in humanity's need to express itself and be appreciative of such expression. But why? I think such a question can only be justified provisionally. Wittgenstein warned of looking to deeply into the reasons behind things. There are times when all one can say is that it is simply so. This is in no way a dismissal of such endeavours, but a simple appreciation of the limits of analytical precision.

27/1/99

I wonder if the Pre-Raphaelites were correct in their insistence that all the arts stemmed from the same fundamental source. Poetry is as expressive of human convictions as is painting, and both are engendered through the same basic human motivations. The painter and the poet are one in their endeavours to express what is essentially inexpressible. They are simply two sides of the same artistic coin. Dante Gabriel Rossetti was perhaps the most successful of the Pre-Raphaelites in his achievements in both the poetic and the visual artistic medium. While perhaps not as successful as William Blake, Rossetti never the less expressed through both outlets a grand sublimity of artistic effusion. One can appreciate the talents of both artists when the poetic proliferations of J. M. W. Turner are considered in comparison. While he was one of the most prolific and esteemed artists of his generation, Turner's poetical endeavours were simply lacking in expressive competency. As with Blake, Rossetti's paintings can only be fully appreciated when viewed in the light of his poetry. Rossetti was of course not as philosophically minded as Blake, and so his paintings are not imbued with the same robust philosophical motifs. Both, however, seemed sure of their emotive faculties and were able to imbue their works with a considerable emotional intensity. Blake through the gestures of the participants in his artistic creations, and Rossetti in his ability to capture the emotional play upon the countenance of a subject. Of course the links between Blake's art and poetry are somewhat closer given the production of his illuminated works. Rossetti paid closer attention to capturing the essence of the female subject, while Blake was more concerned with the portrayal of religious sensibilities. Their artistic voices were shaped upon different cultural canvases, and so the programmatic directions of their respective outputs were different in some marked degree.

28/1/99

I again met Samantha this afternoon, the woman who I initially met at Kylie's birthday dinner. I have to say she is quite a dynamic individual. I have found in the brief time that I have known her that she continually forces you to re-evaluate your priorities. She entreats you to confront the level of intensity with which you live. This can be both exhilarating and quite uncomfortable. It the face of her exuberant embrace upon life you are compelled to consider with greater forthrightness your convictions and most strongly held preconceptions. I find myself questioning the gusto with which I am conducting my life. While I endeavour to squeeze the most out of every day, there must be more that I can do. Where is the intensity of my youth? Can it be a conscious effort that propels one back into the emotional fray? Or do such feeling merely descend once more upon the unsuspecting person? I guess I am sounding like an old man, and when I think of how I lead my life this doesn't necessarily ring true. The depth of feeling that accompanies the reading of a poem is still paramount in my life. The sheer joy of a stroll through the botanical gardens during a summers evening still invigorates the soul. Art and music continue to provide me the emotional stimulation that they always have. I guess when all things are considered, I can't really be charged with emotional complacency. It is perhaps just in relation to Samantha that I feel I am in some way lacking. For the intensity with which she embraces the day is of such a degree that it eclipses the vigour of those who

Diary of a Schizophrenic

pass through her sphere. Such a taste for the emotional lends itself to a higher regard for life in general and serves as beacon to those who lead a less passionate existence. As Whitman releases a barbaric YAWP across the rooftops of the world, so to does this intriguing individual express a yearning for the sap from the tree of life to sweeten the world's consciousness.

30/1/99

We are currently looking at houses into which we might move. There are quite a number of considerations that one must weigh up when choosing a house. Firstly there is the location. The location is indeed crucial, and the right area can enhance a person's lifestyle in no uncertain terms. For instance, tonight we looked at a house just of Rathdowne Street, in North Carlton. The area is superb for small restaurants and café's, and even maintains a small park area. It is however just out of comfortable walking distance of the university, which would mean a short drive each day. This is not to say that a walk is not out of the question, though one would say that the car would be the preferred option. Then there is the condition of the house. This particular house is newly renovated and quite beautiful. I have yet to survey the interior, but by my reckoning it will only do justice to the exterior. So we have a fine house in a good area, with only the inconvenience of having it just out of walking distance from the university; amicable location, upstanding exterior, and unseen interior. There is apparently a small back yard as well. But we must consider all our options. I would not mind living in Middle Park or perhaps Albert Park, though the rent can be quite expensive. Anything that is on the coast is of course very costly, simply in accordance with its location. But I am at a loss to think of anywhere else to live. Carlton, North Carlton, Parkville, or Albert Park seems my immediate preference. As I have matured the character of the house in which I live has become increasingly important. Surroundings do indeed shape a person to some extent, and to be pleased by one's environment lends itself to a congeniality of lifestyle. My mother has in some respects proved this to be true. Her choice of living space always reflects something of herself, lending an ease and comfort to her life.

31/1/99

I have recently been asked to submit a short piece to the magazine *Farrago*. I am currently undecided as to whether I shall attempt to undertake such a task. I think I have in effect made a decision by default. It was Samantha, the lady who I met last Friday night at Kylie's birthday dinner, who requested that I submit the piece. She has been elected editor of the magazine and is quite keen to secure contributions. Not really knowing what I was getting myself into I said that I would indeed submit something. Without having given it much thought, I found myself in a number of meetings with Samantha attempting to formulate what I might write upon. It was decided that I should make comment upon the plight of the classics department and study of the classics in general. While I do enjoy reading the classics, my knowledge of the broader social implications of the current academic plight of studies in classics is indeed quite limited. There seem to me a whole range of various issues which are in question here, and I don't seem to have a good grasp of anything. There is also the question of whether I would like to write for *Farrago* in the first place. I have never really given it much consideration. It's been quite some time since I've read a copy of the magazine, and I would be at a loss to describe to someone its general content. The reading that I have engaged upon has revealed quite a politically biased point of view. I have no wish to become embroiled in any political and ideological dialogues with any of the readership of the magazine. Though when all is considered, I really should put such concerns behind me and at least attempt to write something. Even if I get rejected, then at least I've done what I am in some respects now obliged to do.

Diary of a Schizophrenic

1/2/99

It has become quite evident that I no longer enjoy the same depth of emotion that I once did. During the course of my earlier years I was quite prone to feelings of heightened intensity which furnished my life with a level anxious and melancholic despair. Though this condition was regularly punctuated by moments of blissful religiously inspired serenity. When you are subject to the prevalence of emotional turbulence, there is present in your daily existence an intense awareness of the beauty of life. During the occasional lull in the emotional furore one is able to glimpse the sanctity of the human condition. It is in many respects such insight is like a drug that sustains your existence. Coupled with a certain philosophical propensity, life can maintain an idealistic and romantic fervour. Music, art, poetry, literature, and many of the other noble and artistic pursuits engendered by the human mind are seen in an uncompromising majesty which can indeed nourish the suffering soul. The tumult of daily life on occasion gives way to the splendour of the present moment, in which one is absorbed in sacred union with the infinite in humanity. This can manifest itself in a keenly religious sensibility that cradles the devout in a warm cocoon of security. The religious experience can open the mind of the disciple into worlds of unimaginable bliss, which in turn instil a hallowed revere for the simplicity of the world. Such religious intensity can be viewed with disdain by the uninitiated, and indeed can result is quite unrestrained behavioural modifications that can be shocking to the unreligious. Such tendencies must be treated with a certain respect, if not acceptance, for the newly born spiritualist is susceptible to a fragility of temperament. But even in the face of unremitting opposition, the strength of conviction that is present in the initiate during the initial moment of experience can overcome almost any obstacle. A light has been seen; certitude in the face of unending complicity with life's negativity has been perceived.

2/2/99

I wonder in what manner I should characterise my good friend Jill Gardner. A lady of infinite compassion and considerable intelligence. Her outward beauty only serves to enhance the inner beauty of her soul. I know only that in her company a person can feel entirely at ease. Her manner is self-assured and lacks nothing of the refinement of a well-educated woman. There is little which can be said which does not make extensive use of the superlative. A gentle and kind woman who harbours a certain enthusiasm for the world. Prone to the emotional vicissitudes of a sensitive constitution, she never the less conducts her life in a mature and level-headed fashion. With a keen interest in the psychological, she directs her sharp intellect toward the securing of knowledge. Her religious sensibilities lend a depth of conviction to her actions, and furnish her life with a compassionate heart. With a strong empathic connection to the world, she makes friends easily and maintains them despite the injustices of distance. And her sense of humour! There really is little that can be said other than her sense of fun can be contagious. It revels in a realm of uninhibited abandon that rarely seeks the world for justification. She has known hardship and has triumphed. She harbours deep regrets about her past, but they in no way impede the harmonious running of her present. She is quite passionate about a number of issues, and has been known to follow such inclinations. Without recourse to the restrictive insecurities that can debilitate some, she happily embraces life with a graceful endurance. Unconcerned with the cloistered world of the social hierarchy she leads an existence which is founded in a genuine acceptance of character. I am fortunate to be acquainted with such a passionate creature and am delighted that I can indeed call her friend. Knowing such people gives one a faith in the sanctity of the human condition.

4/2/99

I saw the most thoroughly enjoyable play last night. It was called *Master Class*, and depicted a seminar given by a retired opera singer to group of young operatic performers. The entire play was something of a monologue punctuated by the performances of the singers. The quality of the acting was indeed something special, and the main actress who played the part of the retired diva gave a masterly performance. She imbued the part with a staunch humour that endeared the audience. One could indeed imagine the life of the performer which the play was based upon, the acting was that powerful. The main actress carried the play simply on her own performance. And what's more we were fortunate enough to secure the most incredible seats. They were about five rows back and situated directly in the centre. The action of the play was virtually directed straight toward us. The upper class mannerisms which characterised the performance were done with a consummate ease. I must say I was very impressed. The evening was capped of with a romantic interlude with an old girl friend. It's quite true, it always happens when you least expect it. I have no idea what the consequences of last night will be, but we must wait and see. It's been so long since I have felt the amorous attentions of a lady that I had almost forgotten what it was like. But mostly it was fun to once again engage in a romantic capacity with a beautiful young lady. After the play we took a stroll through the botanical gardens. The evening was pleasantly warm, and the stars were quite visible. We chose a spot, and the sat, proceeding to talk well into the evening. I was quite nervous as it become apparent that something was going to happen romantically, and I felt myself dusting of the cobwebs as it were. But things went very smoothly, and a wonderful evening was enjoyed. It just feels nice to be kissed. The botanical gardens can indeed instil a certain romance into an evening.

5/2/99

It's been so hot over the last few days that my ability to concentrate on what I'm doing has been severely depleted. You are simply sapped of your will, and the most menial tasks take on added difficulty. Even sitting at this computer I am sweating all over the keyboard. I've noticed while writing in this journal that I am not very self-reflexive in regards to my feelings. It seems as if I am contenting myself with analysis such things as literature, the theatre, and the constitution of my friends. I feel I must delve a little deeper in the emotional happenings of my life. What I really feel about the situations which I encounter in my everyday life. But it seems as if I'm not experiencing the same emotional intensity as I once did. Maybe this is simply what happens as you get older. But never the less, I shall endeavour to make more of an account of my feelings in regards to my daily life. I guess my life is fairly stable at the moment – my short-term future being sorted out, and my aims and ambitions still firmly in sight. My time is still occupied with reading mainly, and this provides the satisfaction which sustain my life. I should perhaps attempt to write a little more, though this will come with time. I think you have to reach a certain level of maturity before your writing can truly reflect your life. Perhaps this is just an excuse to postpone writing. It's more a question of deciding what I would like to write upon. A friend of mine is writing a play which has inspired me to perhaps follow my own creative inspirations. I feel I certainly have it in me to write fiction, we will just have to wait and see. It might be that I don't have the emotional range anymore to write effectively. I think you need to feel life with a certain intensity to truly get the most out of your writing. For the time being I'll concentrate on my academic writing, and when I've finished my honours year, I may attempt to write a little more fiction.

6/2/99

I've decided that the only method conducive to the clearest expression of my thoughts and feelings is to write from the heart. Intellectualisation only serves to muddy the waters when one is attempting to detail the complexities of the human soul. No, this statement should be qualified by saying that over-intellectualisation unduly hampers the creative process. The intellect has its place in scheme of things. It should know its place and never attempt to extend its dominion beyond the chartered dictate of its prescribed arena. Meaning should be expressed by means of a clear and uncluttered vocabulary. The most direct avenue should always be chosen from the heart of the writer to the heart of the reader. It is no platitude that the simple and uncomplicated often encapsulates the sublime, and this creed should be closely followed by the aspiring writer. There is little room for the verbose articulation of superfluous rhetoric whose only mandate is to impress the intellect at the expense of the heart. Having said this, it still must be said that a sound grasp of the English language is indeed a prerequisite of precise articulation. If you don't have the words, you are left floundering in an inarticulate void without recourse to the saving graces which a heightened vocabulary can afford the writer. One can be so bedazzled by the power of words, and so in love with their power to move, that one forgets that they are simply a tool for the expression of thought and emotion. But still one must love words – one must fall deeply in love with the subtle variations in expression which words afford the writer. The composition of grammatically correct sentential structures will inevitably take care of itself. One must extend one's vocabulary to eventual transcend it. Words should never be used for heir own sake, only in the pursuit of artistic and scholarly precision should they be employed – with a pure and uninhibited intent.

7/2/99

I really must admire the way Tolstoy constructs a novel. The sheer number of entwining narratives can at times be difficult to follow, but when they are comprehended they really add something special to the story. How he managed to keep track of the various personalities and the differing ways they interact in differing situations is a wonder. The plot of *Anna Karenin* is a vast web of interconnected stories which is woven with the utmost skill. Such a structure does however have the disadvantage of leaving you wondering who your sympathises should lie with. Obviously Anna Karenin is the main protagonist, but she at times takes a back seat to other characters. As soon as one character becomes the main focus, another assumes a central role. This serves to continually introduce new and varying chemistry between the main characters. It's been so long since I've read a novel that it may just possibly be my unfamiliarity with the dynamics of the novel form that leads be to be astounded at such narrative devices by Tolstoy. *Anna Karenin* is brim full with wonderful insight into the workings of the human condition, and the descriptive power of the work is at times startling. Tolstoy however never rests in his strengths, but is always willing to subject the reader to a number of skilfully crafted narrative devices. Description gives way to intensely staged dialogue, and in turn back to description. Reading Tolstoy really inspires me take up the art of fiction for myself. I have no idea whether I can be any good at such a task, but indeed I should try. But I have to read a good deal more fiction that I have been doing, but I can see no difficulty in this. I really enjoy spending the whole day just reading. It's just as of late my interests have been more directed toward the reading of the classics. I will definitely have to take more time to read fiction. And indeed even some modern fiction. It's been some time since I've read anything younger than a year.

8/2/99

I have been asked to submit an article to the *Farrago* team. The subject matter concerns the plight of the classics department and the study of the classics in general. I am finding myself stalling at the commencement of the article. I guess I am still undecided as to whether I really want to write it. *Farrago* is such a political biased magazine that I really don't want to become embroiled in any political wrangling. If I was to write the article I would endeavour to make it as apolitical as possible. Though as I think about it, this isn't really possible. I would have to question the current academic emphasis on degrees for job placement rather than personal enrichment. It follows that this would involve a discussion of the current political climate. But never the less, I think there is still a valid point to be made in favour of a greater emphasis being placed upon things such as studies of the classics. The question must be asked, "What is the value of an education?" It seems such an obvious point to start. Should we be concerned with the facilitation of employment, or should we rather put the emphasis on personal development. Or indeed, can a balance be struck between the two. The classics themselves are something more than just a matter of taste. Contained within those ancient pages is a veritable trove of fundamental insights into the nature of the human condition. If one lives by the dictate "know thyself", then a study of the classics can yield an endless store of self-reflexive inspiration. There are times when I've looked in the mirror and thought how poignant Ovid's story of Narcissus is. If had not been for a sound grasp of the classics, T. S. Eliot would not have even contemplated *The Wasteland*, and James Joyce would definitely have not conceived of *Ulysses*. These are only two examples of the power which the classics exert upon the modern world. Freud found undeniable inspiration in the story of Oedipus, using the classic tale to augment his psychological insight. And the list goes on of instances where a knowledge of the classics has lead to cultural invigoration.

9/2/99

I have been conceiving a number of ideas for a novel. The main protagonist will be a young man in his early twenties who embarks upon a spiritual journey through the sacred dictates of Buddhism and into the realms of shamanism. In many respects it shall be an autobiographical account, but with a fictitious narrative. I shall draw upon the experiences which I encountered when I am become interested in Buddhism. The story will begin at the university where the young man first encounters the teachings of Buddhism in a series of lectures. It will then trace his brief but intense relationship with a young woman who he meets a dinner party. As the relationship unfolds, the young man is continually forced to reconcile his burgeoning spirituality. While in the process of experimenting with abstency, he meets another woman with whom he falls for. A love quadrangle ensues, as it turns out that the new woman, the current beau and a second man have known each other and have been involved in respective relationships. Throughout the course of all of this, the young man decides to give in to his new found spiritualism, and embark upon a close study of Buddhism. He relinquishes both his newfound love and his current girl friend, and finds a Buddhist teacher who may show him the way. As a result of his inquiries the young man confronts a number of deep and startling spiritual insights. His spiritual quest, however, takes an unexpected turn, as he is forced to confront an unremitting dark night of the soul (as described by Saint John of the Cross). Emerging from the months of spiritual deprivation, and on the verge of a strengthened faith in Buddhism, the young becomes prone to a Kundalini crisis, and is once again forced to confront the darker side of himself. The crisis shears him of all confidence and leaves him struggling with its immense power. I'm not certain how I will end the story, but that is the essence of the story line. It obviously needs a good deal of fleshing out, but I think the structure is there for quite a compelling narrative.

10/9/98

It's becoming increasingly apparent that I want to try my hand at fiction. A certain dream has been forming deep within the emotive recesses of my mind. That dream is to retire to the country for an extended period and write a book. In fact it may be some time before I am afforded the opportunity to live in the country, so I may just have to content myself with the writing of a book. More and more my thoughts wander through that fertile bed of literary inspiration, and I am left to lead my life in the knowledge that this is where my true vocation lies. It is now my responsibility to acquire as much insight into the craft of writing fiction as is possible. Some think the art of writing fiction can be taught others consider it inherently inspirational. I am sure that there is an element of both. With any luck I shall have a small amount of talent with which to work, and so may endeavour to improve my abilities with intensive study. I see no reason why I shouldn't get something published, as my command of the English language is indeed of a level to warrant such aspirations.

Diary of a Schizophrenic

Admittedly, it does require a good deal of work, but nothing which is impossible. I enjoy writing, and reading has been the main stay of my life throughout my adulthood, so I seem to maintain the established and traditional ingredients of success. Writing requires a dogged determination and a persistence in the face of constant rejection; traits I feel I possess. I enjoy my own company, which is an asset to the life of a writer, who inevitably must spend long periods in isolation for the sake of literature. I have always been quite solitary, so this should not pose a problem. I haven't written much fiction during the past few years, so I am certain that I shall be somewhat rusty, though this in no way deters me. If it is something that I truly wish to do, then there shan't be any obstacle too large to overcome. I am filled a true desire to become a writer.

11/2/99

Can this be all there is to life? Am I leading life of fully realised integrity and unrestrained intensity? My days are spent pouring over various works of literature and philosophy, and I must say that I wouldn't have it any other way. I introduce a certain variety in my chosen habitations by perhaps reading in the treasury gardens under an old oak tree, or investing some time in the philosophy library. My time is divided between the university and home, and I am quite content for it to be so. There is just so much to do in preparation for the upcoming year that I should rarely have a moment to spare. I have made significant inroads into the material that I am required to read, so I feel I am something ahead of schedule. I must admit, the scholarly life does hold much appeal for me. Libraries are sacred places for me, allowing me to indulge in unmitigated binges of reading, without concern for life or limb. But do such inclinations give me the fullest possible satisfaction from a day? I can think of no better way to spend a day than to wile it away in the comforting confines of the philosophy library at the university. It is a wonderfully conducive environment for the exercising of true scholarly acumen. The book lined walls, and the scholarly discourse which pervades the scene, all contribute to an aura of learned revere. My heart is full of the sincerest admiration for those noble souls who toil away in the recesses of the worlds libraries compiling and propagating knowledge – no matter in what field. Of course my preference is for English or philosophy, and to spend a day in library, the topic of research must be concerned with either of these two pursuits. I had a splendid time at the Fitzwilliam Museum in Cambridge when I was granted permission to view an originate copy of William Blake's *Marriage of Heaven and Hell*. The room which housed the volume cradled me as if I was a newborn babe, providing a warmth and comfort which contributed to the pleasure of perusing the aforementioned volume. To secure paid employment within such environs would truly be a pleasure.

12/2/99

I really should endeavour to compose a good deal more poetry. I have a certain knack for the expression of poetic contrivances, and I should indulge this talent more frequently. No I wouldn't call it a talent; it's more of a poetic affinity with the use of words. I still haven't found my poetic voice as of yet. I have an inkling of what it may entail, but I have been unable to fully realise it. I have a feeling that it maintains a didactic sensibility, though my poetry of late teaches little and informs less. I am still experimenting with creating a flexible poetic vocabulary. I find myself continually constrained by what I have already written. I need to continually reinvent the poetic structures that uphold my work, so as not to become constrained by them. I am yet to strike the balance between technique and creative flair. Some poems are overly concerned with poetic forms, metre, and rhyme, while others are more concerned with the image, figure and conceits of the poem. It is something of a juggling act to balance all these considerations in producing a poem. You can't let the creative impetus be curtailed by structural considerations, while at the same time there needs to be an inherent awareness of such structures for the poem

Diary of a Schizophrenic

to realise its full potential. I would say that writing poetry is perhaps the most demanding form of writing, and there is so little time to express what needs to be said, and it never the less needs to be expressed in an articulate and clear fashion. Strange as it might seem to say, writing poetry for me is rarely about expression of particular feelings, it is more about exercising the possibilities of poetic form. I have trouble articulating specific thoughts in the poetic form, and must instead content myself with holding a particular idea before my mind as I write in unconstrained fashion. This seems to shape the poem in the particular direction in which I wish it to take, while allowing me the expressive flexibility of an unconscious stream of thought. Not all my poems are produced in such a manner, though most of the most interesting seem to be.

15/2/99

I am overcome by a certain apathetic acceptance of the monotony of existence. I fail to find the smallest joy in what was once a surging fountain of rapturous delight. I am certain that such a condition is only temporary, though such knowledge is of cold comfort for the present as I labour under this melancholic disposition. I have just spent an evening with friends, and could find little solace in the comforting embrace of their company. I treasure my friends beyond measure and the many and varied interactions of their lives provide the well-spring of my happiness. It's just that tonight I lie beyond the reach of friendly consolation. It is an apathy of the greatest degree that so ensnares my soul, and I can but subsist under its unyielding weight. I know it shall pass as a light shower gives way to the suns rays on a summer's afternoon. Still, I rejoice at the variety which life provides. This is what is so invigorating about the human condition, that it can contain such diversity of emotion. To be overcome by the meaningless despondency of life is to participate in an almost divine acceptance of humanity. It all meets in a crescendo of emotive transcendence that provides life with its intensity. It is only during those moments when we are stripped bare and left to swing on the harrowing breeze of existence, do we truly come to understand ourselves and the all that life entails. True happiness is only possible after an extended voyage into the darkest recess of the mind. Only when one has come to terms with the meaninglessness of life can its true poignancy become apparent. Some try their best to avoid such paradoxical truth, constructing their lives upon the shifting sands of habituation, hoping to hide from the wrath of life so as to avoid the pain which leads to eventual rebirth. Alexander Pope identified such people in his poem "An Elegy to the Memory of an Unfortunate Lady." They but peep out once an age, never hearing the full symphony of life.

16/2/99

It is getting quite close to the time when I begin my honours year, and my anticipation is growing by the day. I have prepared well and am looking froward to a successful year. But time is proceeding at such a rate that I am confounded. It is something of a platitude to say that time accelerates as one gets older, and I am definitely experiencing the pace. When life proceeds with a certain rhythm, the days pass buy at such a rate that is almost inconceivable, especially when one is busy and meaningfully engaged. So it is half way through February, and March is about to commence, and before a word can be uttered in disbelief it will be December and the new millennium will be dawning. All one can do is make the most of each day as it presents itself, and try not to become to overwhelmed by habitual tendencies. The great thing about time moving so quickly is that I am reading a good deal of material in what seems no time at all. I have already read all the books in the philosophy library pertaining to my thesis, and have compiled quite a lengthy bibliography already. I am also able to read a deal of fiction and poetry on top of what I am reading for my studies, so it goes without saying that my days are consumed by the act of reading. But I would not have it any other way. There is just so much to read in such a small amount of time that it exasperates the mind just thinking about it. I am cultivating a strong passion for fiction, though I am still well and truly enamoured by the classics. I think I will compromise and start reading classic novels, thereby easing my self into fiction from the realms of epic poetry and drama. I would love to read some modern drama, as well as exposing myself to a greater range of biography. The lives of the great artists, poets, and composers hold a special fascination for me. One can see in their lives the normalcy that propelled genius, thereby giving inspiration to one's own life.

18/2/99

I had a coffee with a friend this morning, and as it turned out we talked for almost two hours. I am amazed at how interested she is in the interactions of her friends. Their daily lives and the extent to which they impinge upon her life are thoroughly analysed and considered to the last detail. I just have the pleasure of sitting back and enjoying the various stories as they unfold. She is exasperated at their trials, and joyous in their triumphs. I often wonder how I am portrayed when she talks with another of her friends. While I am keenly interested in the goings on of my acquaintances, I guess I look to extrapolate a little more upon the lessons which are learnt from the interactions of my friends. I guess I am not as exposed to as wide a range of humanity as she is, so am more content to talk of other things rather than the trials and tribulations of my closest companions. Maybe I am simply less sensitive to other people. That is to say perhaps I do not allow other people to have quite the impact on my life. I'm not sure whether this is curse or a blessing, but I guess it shows quite a strong independence on my part. But perhaps I wish I were a little more involved with people, as she is. I really value my solitude too much to compromise it with a continued exposure to a large group of people. I find I am striking quite a nice balance at the moment between the time I am able to afford myself, and the time which I spend with friends. I am little less solitary, though more content to spend time by myself when the opportunity presents itself.

19/2/99

Though I am enthusiastic as ever about the prospect of commencing my honours year, I never the less would enjoy nothing more than taking an entire year to learn the finer points of the craft of writing. I would entirely devote myself to the acquisition of knowledge regarding the art of writing fiction. I would read as many books on the craft as have been written. I would read fiction voraciously, never ceasing to explore the limitless range of its potential. I would even go so far as to read a dictionary, and would endeavour to come to terms with English grammar. Mornings would be set aside for the sole purpose of writing, while afternoons would be spent reading. Firstly I would write short fiction to hone my skills, but after a year or so I would embark upon the writing of a novel. To have a "work in progress" would provide me with the greatest joy and satisfaction. To be creating something, to be involved in the construction of a piece of literature, would I think would be very fulfilling. I think essentially I am a creative person who needs the expressive outlet of some form of artistic pursuit to fully realise happiness. It is now only a matter of discovering if I have any talent in regards to writing. I have been quite successful academically, but this is no indication of any discernable aptitude in the writing of fiction. I need time to develop the range of my expressive capacities, and only then will I be in a position to properly assess if I have any future as a writer. I think if one gets into the habit of writing and becomes familiar with the process, then it can come as naturally as the parlance of the spoken word. I shall have to give myself time though. This is the key, persistence and endeavour in the face of great odds. Most people have a story to tell it's just a matter of having the boldness to tell it. They say everyone has a least one good book in them, well I now I've got a wealth of experience from which to draw, its just a matter if I have the skill to compile it into a work of fiction.

Diary of a Schizophrenic

21/2/99

Yesterday evening I attended a free concert given by the Melbourne Symphony Orchestra at the Sidney Myer Music Bowl. My friend Christine Alexander accompanied me. As it turned out, I didn't really have the opportunity to listen too much of the performance. Christine was very late, and so I waited for her arrival well into the start of the show. When she was more than hour late I decided to go in and see the performance without her. As it turned out, she had arrived just after I had gone in. So we ended up meeting fortuitously at a food stand inside the grounds of the bowl. We then proceeded to talk for the rest of the recital, so I really didn't hear much of it all. I was able to catch a few of Tchaikovsky's more famous phrases, which pleased me immensely. I guess I simply enjoyed Christine's company, though to listen to the music a little more avidly would have been nice. Christine gives one good value in a conversational sense. She is currently writing a play, which I admire. The subject matter of the play is quite bizarre, which details the life of a man who sells his son for fifty dollars. I will have to wait and see a draft of the finished work before I form any judgements. It may well work, and indeed it is a novel and original story.

22/2/99

Something quite perplexing has just occurred. This afternoon I have received a phone call from Samantha, who you may recall me mentioning in a number of my journal entries. It seems as if she is quite serious about me contributing something to the upcoming edition of *Farrago*. I was almost in a mind to forget about the entire affair, and concentrate on my preparations for the upcoming year. Her insistence has however steeled me to the task at hand, and I now shan't shirk the matter. I will summon all the literary acumen at my disposal and produce a piece that will be rival to none in clarity and succinct expression. What I found most surprising however, was the invitation which she afforded me to come and visit her new abode in Carlton. I dare not think of what her intentions may possibly be, though I have to say that I am a little intrigued and somewhat excited at the prospect. At our last meeting I was assured that her intentions where purely to procure my services as a writer and contributor to her magazine. Could I possibly have been mistaken? We struck up an immediate friendship at our first meeting, as we both have a number of things in common. I was quite impressed with her manner and obvious intelligence, and had though that I had likewise impressed her. Our repour at that first encounter was quite free and unconstrained, and I was hopeful that further encounters with her would ensue. And now she calls again, after not having spoken with her for almost a month! I am still wary of her motives, and I shan't expose my heart too openly, though I am pleasantly exited by the whole affair. She is a very dynamic individual with a highly attenuated sense of literary poignancy. She revels, as I do, in a passionate embrace of literature. Her intelligence is unwavering, and she is very attractive. I would never consider that such a woman could have the slightest interest in me, though I wait for our meeting with some anticipation.

23/2/99

Another day of house hunting! Though on this occasion I feel that I have finally found the place in which I wish to reside. The property has a small garden in the front with a few small trees and some delicate little flowering plants. The front windows are stained glass, with even a round portal type window adorning the wall of the front bedroom. The front door opens into a short corridor with polished floorboards. On the left is the main bedroom, and immediately of the right is the secondary bedroom. Both rooms are quite small, though I would say cosy, rather than pokey. The hallway then brings the guest into the main living area, which in turn runs into the dinning room. The main bedroom, and both the living and dining areas contain fireplaces which have been closed, though their façades have been maintained. It gives a warm feel to these rooms. The kitchen adjoins the dining area, and is quite modern in

Diary of a Schizophrenic

its design. A very nice view is afforded from the kitchen area into the backyard, which is paved with a high density of foliage along the fence line. The backyard contains a small shed for the storage of tools and gardening implements. It is indeed a pleasant space for the entertaining of guests, as it is quite spacious, while the trees provide the perfect backdrop, without cluttering up the space. The bathroom follows on from the kitchen, and again is quite modern.

24/2/99

It has been a very eventful few days. On Tuesday night I accompanied my new friend Samantha to a bar in the city where one of her new housemates (she has recently moved) was holding birthday drinks. The conversation was indeed stimulating and without intellectual respite. The topics broached included Chomsky, Wittgenstein, politics, student-academic relationships and of course television. Most people who attended the function were studying in some capacity; most having completed an honours year or commencing a masters degree. During the course of the evening I had the good fortune of conversing with an acutely intelligent woman, who I had to the definite sense that she was interested in me. She is enrolled to commence a masters degree at Melbourne University. We talked briefly and got along famously. I had to employ the full extent of my intellectual acumen to engage in a conversation with her, though the effort was well rewarded. Well the rest of the time at the bar proceeded without incident. I gave Samantha a lift back to her apartment, at which time she invited me inside for an ice cream. We talked until one thirty in the morning, and as I left we briefly kissed. It was quite a pleasant experience, though I have to say she wasn't overly enthusiastic. So I left in a state of consternation. At any rate, I say her again today at the *Farrago* launch party. We talked only briefly, and I had the distinct impression that she was ignoring me. As it turned out, the other woman (I don't yet know her name) from the Tuesday night was in attendance. We talked at some length about a whole host of issue, and even embarked upon something of a philosophical conversation (it's been so long!). Again we got along very well. And the look she gave me upon her departure! If I could but tell of that expression, it simply melted my heart. Unfortunately she left without me learning her name or getting her phone number. The only way I can get into contact with her is to ask Samantha to find her number for me, though this seems impossibility. I was left bewildered at Samantha's behaviour towards me, and it is quite obvious that she holds no feelings for me at all. I can quite happily leave with this, though I am still disconcerted at her attitude towards me. I only hope I meet the other woman once again. Maybe fate will play a hand.

1/4/99

I must apologise for the inordinate length of time which has elapsed since my last entry into this journal. I have been otherwise engaged in considerations of a scholarly nature. I have decided to devote the great majority of my time to the acquisition of knowledge to further the proficiency of my honours year, and so have been unable to a lot time to other things, such as writing in this very journal. Since my last journal entry, I have indeed completed the article that I shall submit to the *Farrago* team for inclusion in their reputable magazine. I have written it under the pseudonym of William MaCrae in order to conceal from my future literary integrity the shameful revelation of an immature style and diction. I thoroughly enjoyed the writing of the article, through which I feel I have identified my true vocation in life, namely to be a writer. Besides my infatuation with the written word, there resides in my breast a fervent desire to propagate the world with literary accomplishments. I feel my entire being has been constructed so as to further my ambitions to such ends. My reticent nature, love of solitude, inalienable desire for knowledge and general bookish sensibilities inexorably lend themselves to the writing life. It still remains a question whether I have any proficiency toward such ends, but in such matters only time will tell. I can only embark upon the journey without neither thought nor head of the possibility of failure. The world will judge me upon the merits of my words. So whether they are full of worth or devoid of meaning, I can do little but begin my intrepid adventure with the thought of success securely implanted in my mind.

3/4/99

It seems to me that the art of writing is a continual struggle between the dictates of inspiration and the demands of technique. T. S. Eliot gave voice to this insight in his critical work "Tradition and the Individual Talent." when he remarked upon the conflict between the conscious and unconscious awareness evident in the creative process. The immature writer is perhaps conscious were he should be unconscious and unconscious were he should be conscious, whereas the great writer is in complete harmony with regards to these creative forces. One must endeavour to give form to the productions of the inspiration through a highly refined sense of the technical. If technique is unduly emphasised however, then the creative impetus is constricted and can but wheeze into life a piece of fiction. And additionally, if the unconscious is purely left to its own devices then the work produced will be of an incoherent nature. A certain balance must be maintained so as to ensure a harmonious synergy between the competing influences. The greatest literary achievements transcend this struggle through a dialectical synthesis which results in a unity of form. As a consequence, the author's intention is subsequently invigorated by possibilities that were unforeseen at the time of composition, and so the work comes to be imbued with broader literary implications. Hence talk of intentionally in the great authors is something of a misnomer, for there certainly is intention in the composition of their works, but that intention is supplanted by the synthetic and dialectical nature of the creative process. The work takes on a life of its own, detached from the mind that has created it. It lives and breathes with the power of this mystical process that has created it, and exists as a child might after the trauma of a birth.

Paul Fearne

21/12/99

As the end of the century approaches with a forceful gusto, I sit down to my typewriter to muse of a life, still in its formative stages, and yet displaying signs of portentous potentiality. At the outset, I will make my ambitions clear. To revolutionise the use of the English language. Many have gesticulated in a similarly pompous and egoist fashion, and I make no claim that such anti-adumbrations are in anyway flattering to the ear. Indeed, as I write these bombastic words, I cringe at the very thought of their general dissemination. But those who never dare to succeed upon the wings of audacious magnanimity will forever languish in the abyss of rectitude. While an ugly apparition to the polite and the sensible, the productions of super-egoist are frequently the most inspired flights of literary and philosophic genius known to humanity. Milton, while composing *Paradise Lost*, was fully aware that he was creating a work of unparalleled sublimity. Rousseau, similarly, thought of himself as perhaps the greatest writer, if not the greatest man, ever to have broached a net. Byron, Shelly, even Blake, embarked upon their literary adventures with a single thought continually militating in their fertile minds, "I will conquer like none have done so before." Forget history, their achievement lies in this one thought. If none of them had written a single salutary word, their immortality would have been secured. The crossroads of time are littered with the corpses of the timid. To try and fail is disaster. To try and fail with a superlative ready at the bow is to conquer the immensities of eternity. (Ah Blake would have definitely approved of that turn of phrase). Any who know me would find such words perplexing , but life and letters rarely sleep in the same bed.

25/12/99

After a very agreeable lunch gorging my highly attenuated sense of taste at Red Rooster's I sat down with a glass of wine to read Paul Johnson's book *Intellectuals*. His effluent moralising is a delight to cringe at. The immensely gratuitous barbarism of person-hood that Johnson takes

Diary of a Schizophrenic

issue with can be described as nothing less that and a triumph of the antinomian and base over the rectitudinal influences of close minded secular pompoustry. To read of the vile intransigence that many of history's intellectuals embraced life steels my soul to the worth of society's more depraved inclinations. One must be careful voicing such views, which are acceptable in the realm of intellectual abstraction, but when given space to operate in the lives of people leads to an abominable lethargy of consciousness, which in turn results in repugnantly course behaviour. What others called depraved, I call human. Consider the sterile adumbration that awaits a world devoid of the lascivious contumely.   Languid, insipid, unspeakably rank and unforgivable dull. My own life has seen a decidedly fervourous attack upon the once secure bastion of conservative magnanimity. After living my teenage years with a firm grasp on the marrow (as it were), I lapsed into a period of rampant conservatism, from which I am only now emerging, thanks to the inspiration of my intellectual forebear's. But I must break of this diversion into my life history, as my housemate has decided to play her music at something above the acceptable levels.

www.ingramcontent.com/pod-product-compliance
Ingram Content Group UK Ltd.
Pitfield, Milton Keynes, MK11 3LW, UK
UKHW041411180426
11947UKWH00007B/66